Annie Marie Musselman

FINDING TRUST

KEHRER

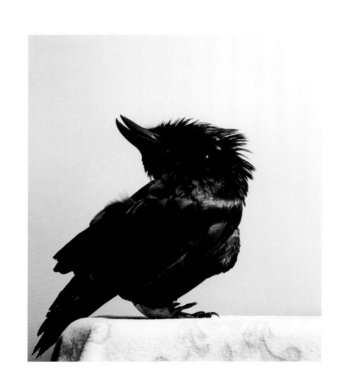

Annie Marie Musselman

FINDING
TRUST

KEHRER

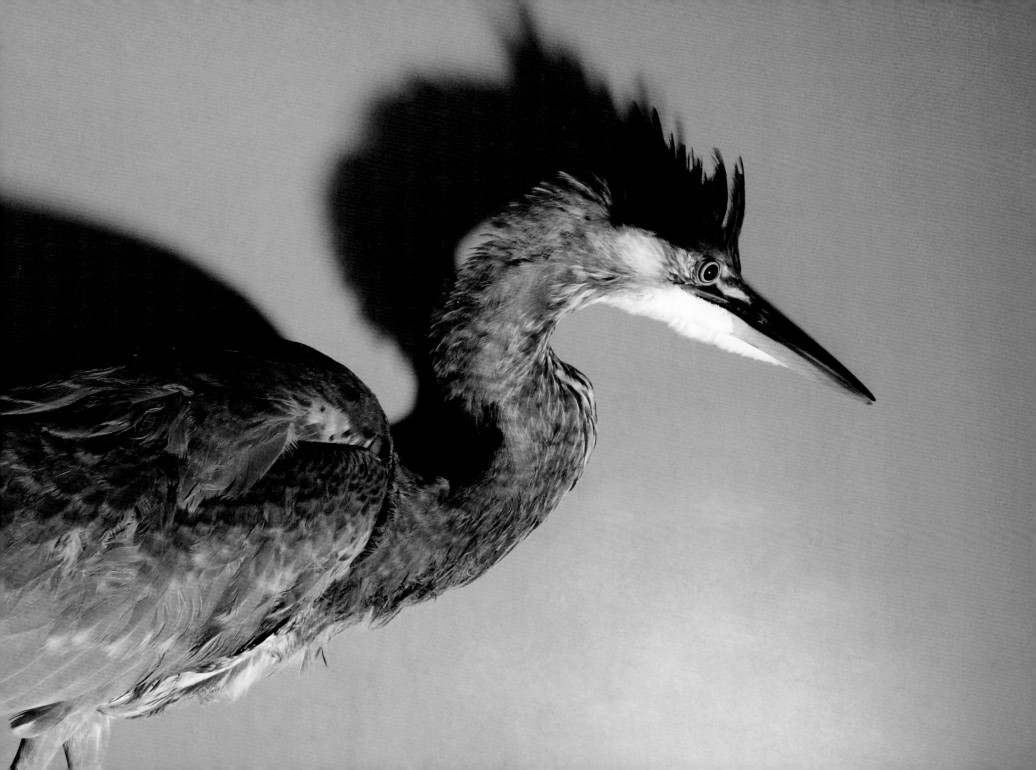

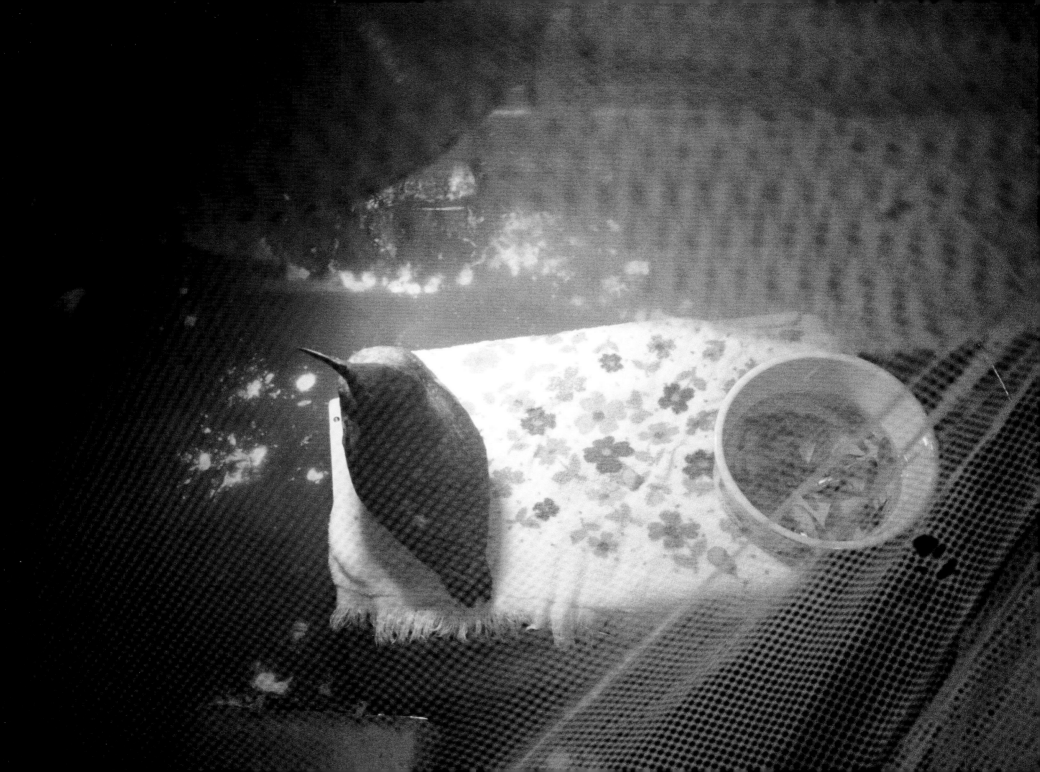

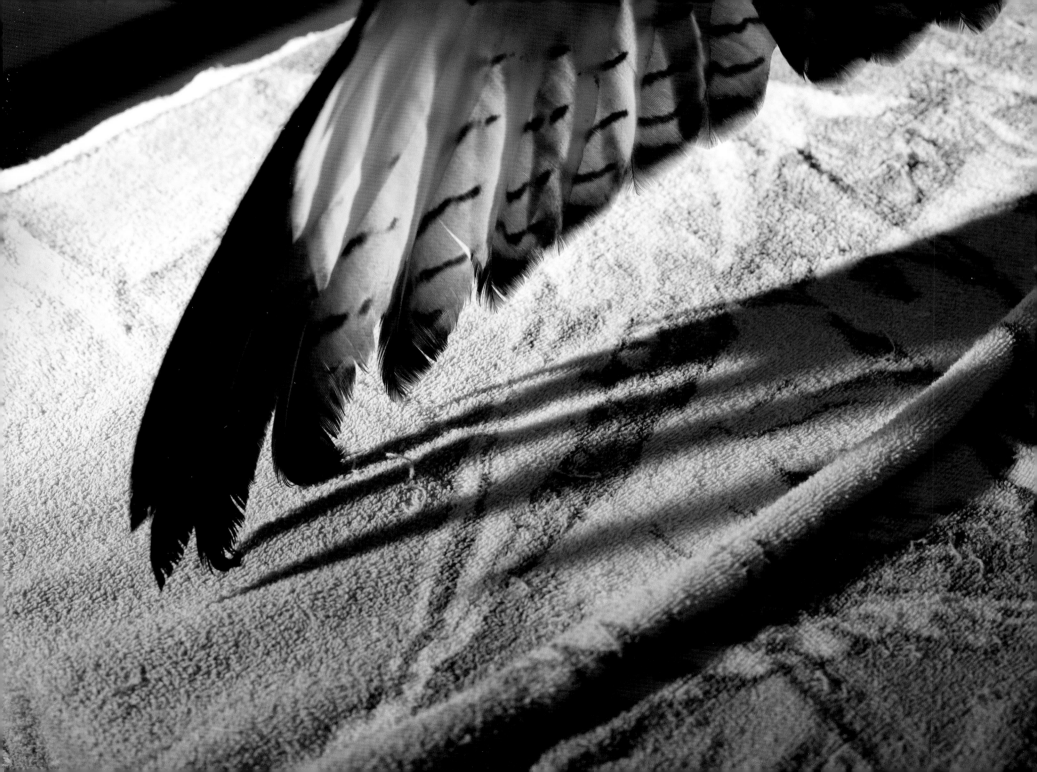

GIVING BACK

It's true that to reach particular material goals in life requires a certain single-mindedness that can leave little time for other experiences. »Look out for number One« or »Keep your eyes on the prize« and »Just do it« are a few of the reminders of where our focus should be. On the other hand, there are those among us who look at life a bit differently, employing their altruistic gene and spending less time on their own program while devoting themselves to the needs of not only our species, but to those of other animals as well. Their rewards are not measured in bank accounts and stock portfolios as much as they are in a feeling of emotional and intellectual fullfillment that comes from helping other beings recover their health and vitality.

I have to believe that exercising this capacity for altruistic behavior provides a unique benefit to our own mental and physical health. We know that pets of all sorts have been a part of the human experience for tens of thousands of years and it is clear that this is so because of the emotional reciprocity that exists between ourselves and our dogs, cats and other companions for example. We do indeed savor the unconditional affection we receive from such animals in our lives.

We expect the veterinarian to invest his or her energies into treating injured animals but what is it that compels some of us to help another species without expecting any economic compensation for our act? Why have members of my household involuntarily intervened when we saw our house cat stalking a fledgling robin, or assisted a confused mole seeking to cross a biking trail

and later cradled a stunned towhee until it recovered its faculties and could fly off? What was in it for us? The answer to these questions are not easily articulated but there is little doubt in my mind that we identified with the struggles of the vulnerable and the injured and their »rights« to get on with their lives. Our empathy towards other life, no matter how small and remote from human contact, reinforced our sense of interrelatedness to the community of life around us.

Until recently, science has been dismissive or indifferent to the intelligence and feelings of other species. For the most part we viewed other species as creatures of instance and the wise and emotional animal was a subject of myth rather than fact. Today however, in part because of the vast array of brain research on other animals we now know unequivocally that higher order vetebrates in particular possess cerebral and emotional capacities not unlike our own. For example, while the brains of some birds are configured differently than those of mammals, they are nevertheless very sophisticated. Members of the crow family use tools, apply insight to solve problems, and experience emotional grief and pleasure. Like us they recognize individual faces, hold grudges, and employ complex family social arrangements.

In her book, Annie Marie Musselman has assembled a collection of unique images of animals that are all in some state of need and in the process of rehabilitation. The photographer's keen eye is our window into the lives of these animals and we immediately begin to identify with their struggles. Some of them will survive and some will not, but there are emotions at play here and Musselman has been able to convey their implicit messages to us free of any heavy-handed emphasis on pain or suffering that can seem contrived.

This collection gives us an insight into that edge of existence that many animals face where humankind and nature collide. This is different from the polished and serene images of nature that we typically view which unintentionally leave us feeling that all is well in the wild world. These are moments caught by an extraordinarily perceptive photographer that help us strengthen our capacity to care for lives not necessarily independent of our own.

All religions include something of an edict that challenges us to treat kindly the life around us. Much of this doctrine suggests that collectively the community of living things is in itself a being greater than ourselves. Our empathy and altruistic response to other animals in need is part of our behavioral link with nature. So equipped we ourselves can be sustained and flourish more fully in the world around us.

Tony Angell — Artist and Naturalist

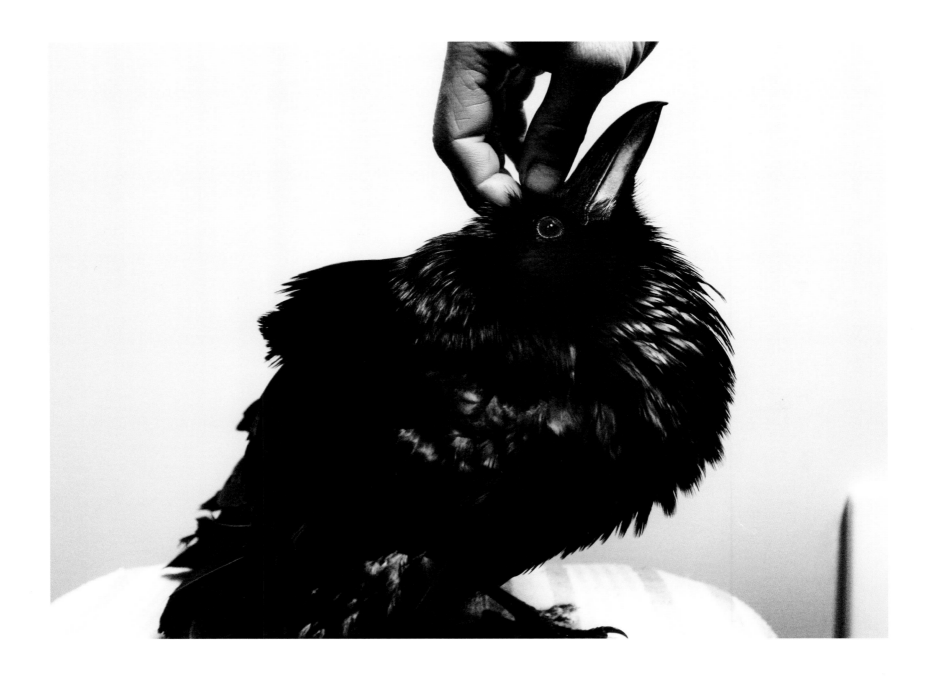

Angel with Jim

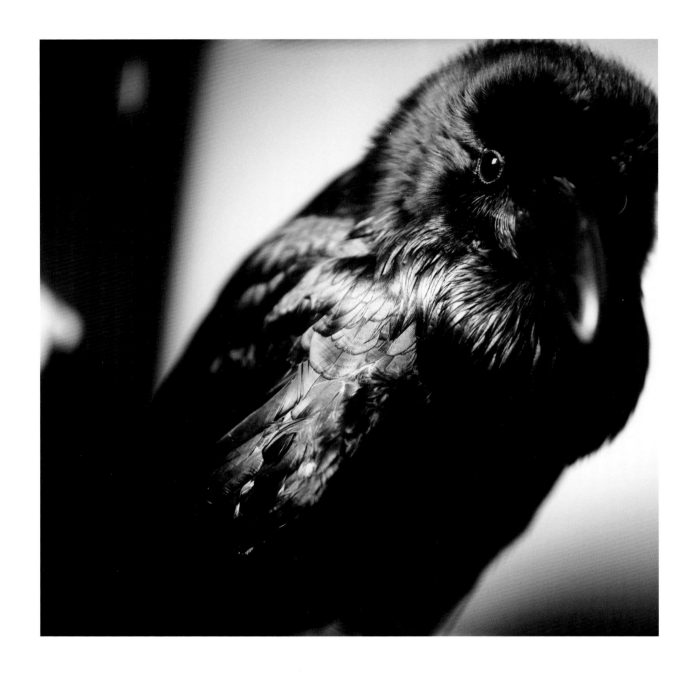

Angel

Angel in Front of Cleaning Towel

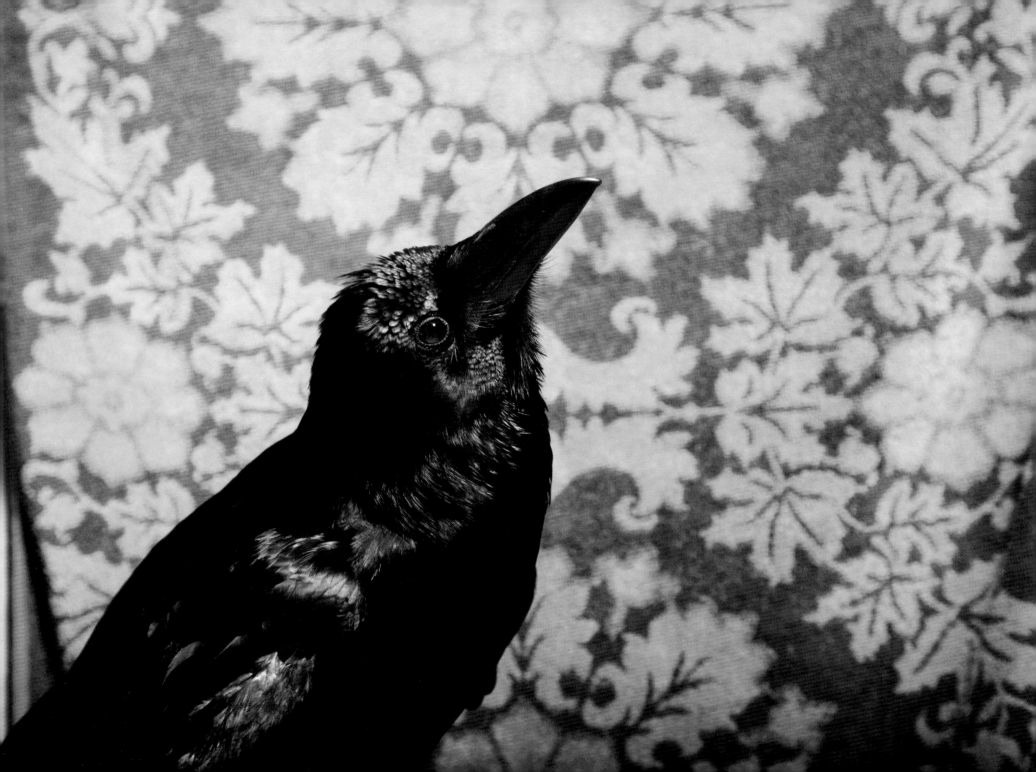

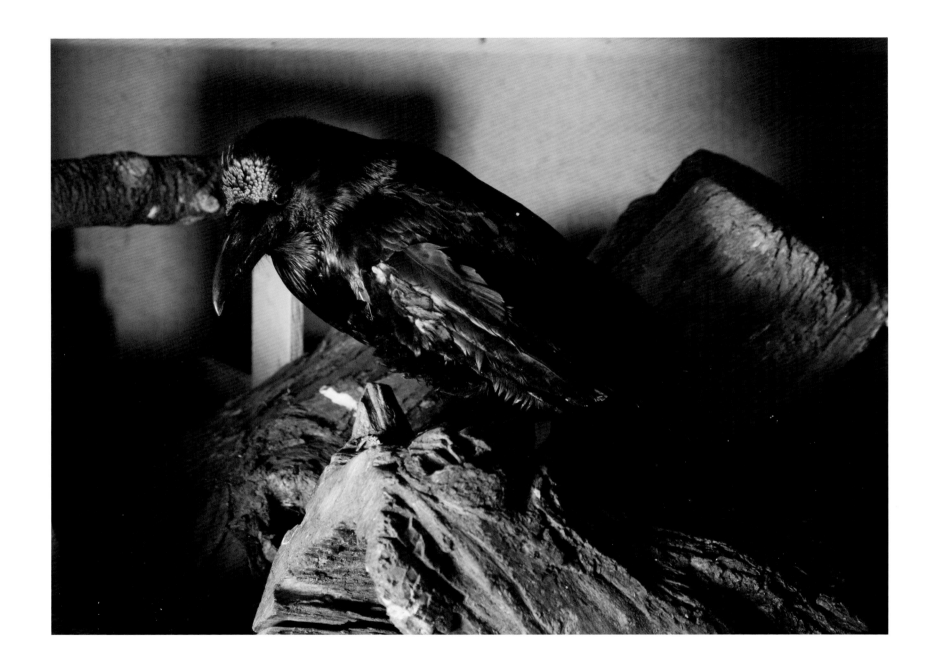

Angel beneath the Eagle Cage

Angel Asleep beneath the Eagle Cage #2

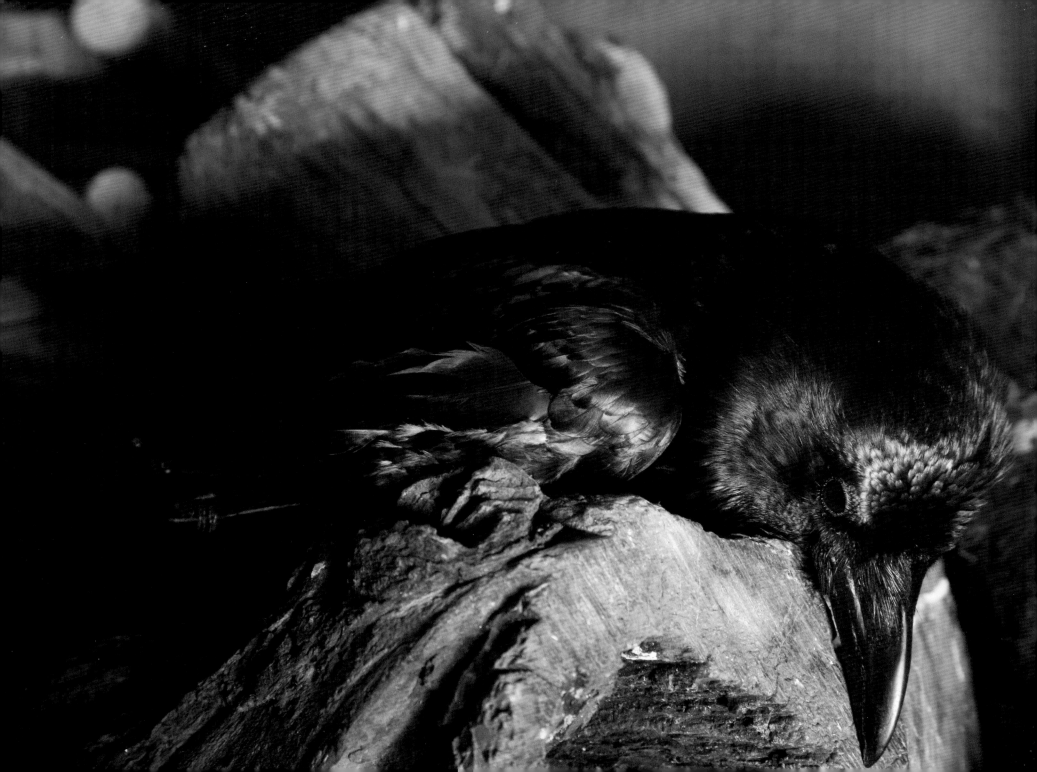

Skaska, Merlin

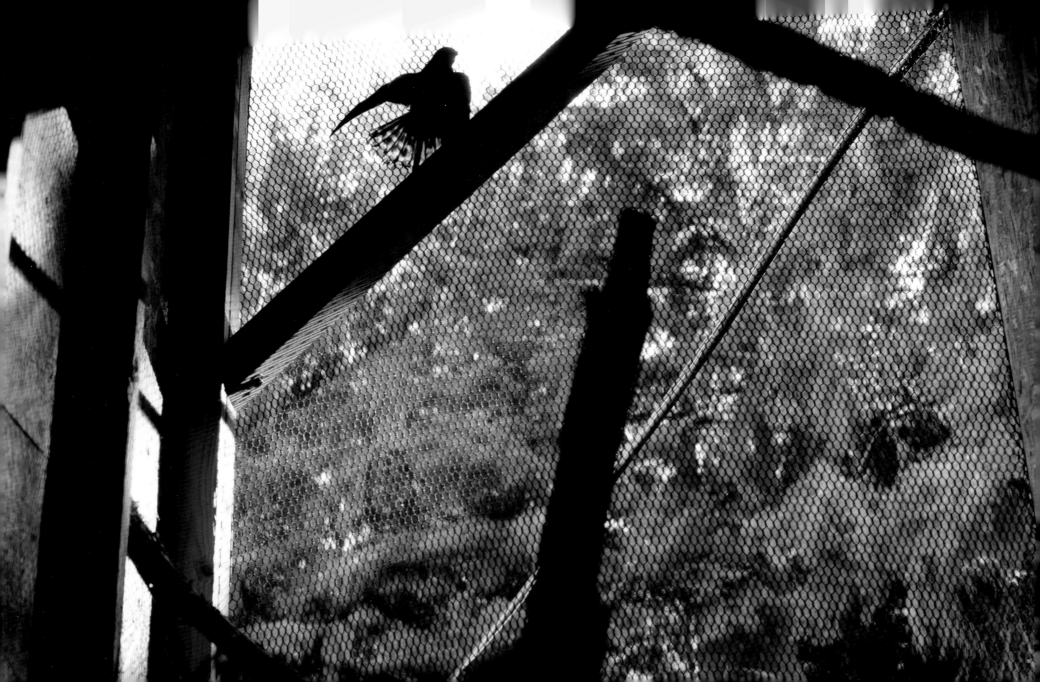

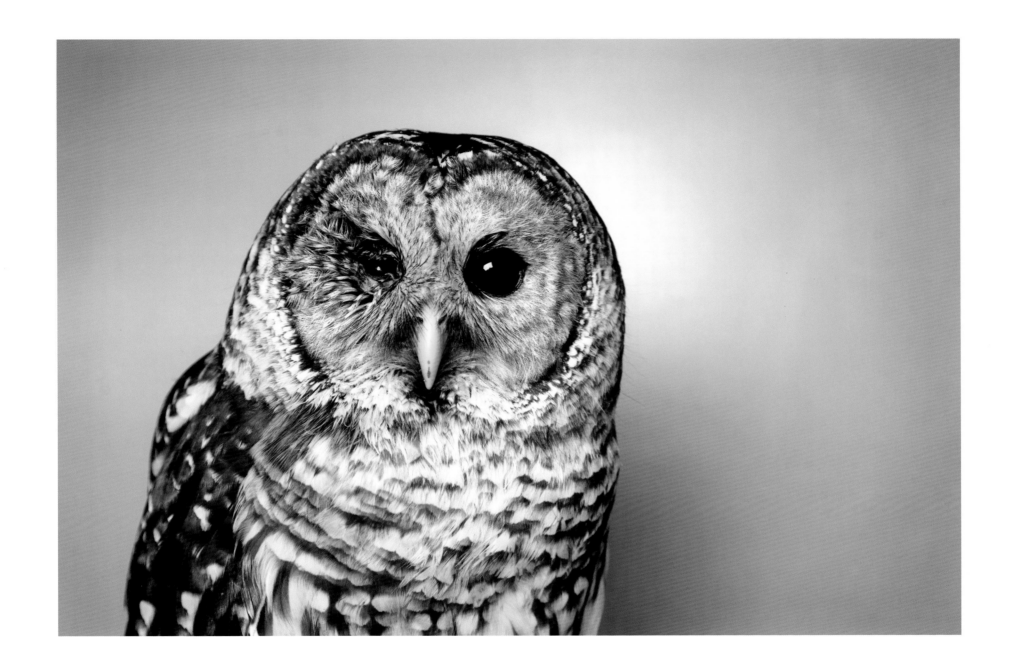

Barred Owl with Eye Damage

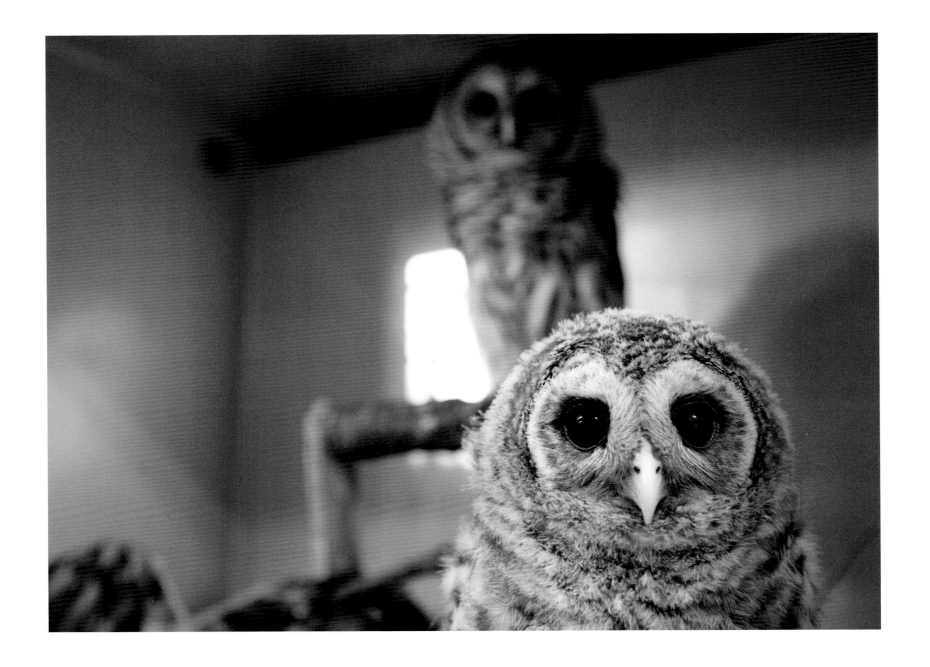

Two Juvenile Barred Owls

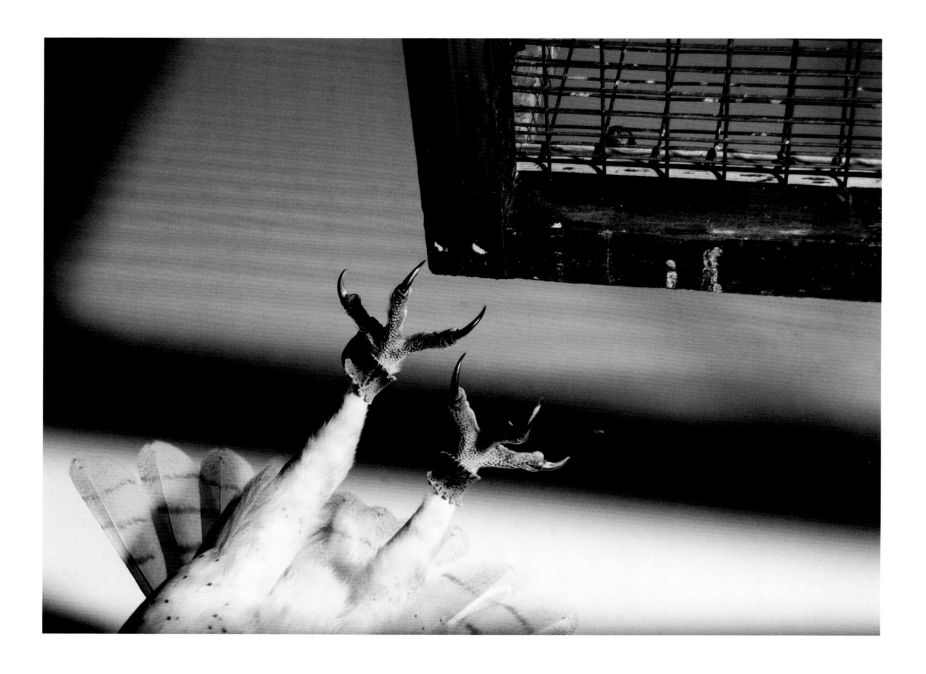

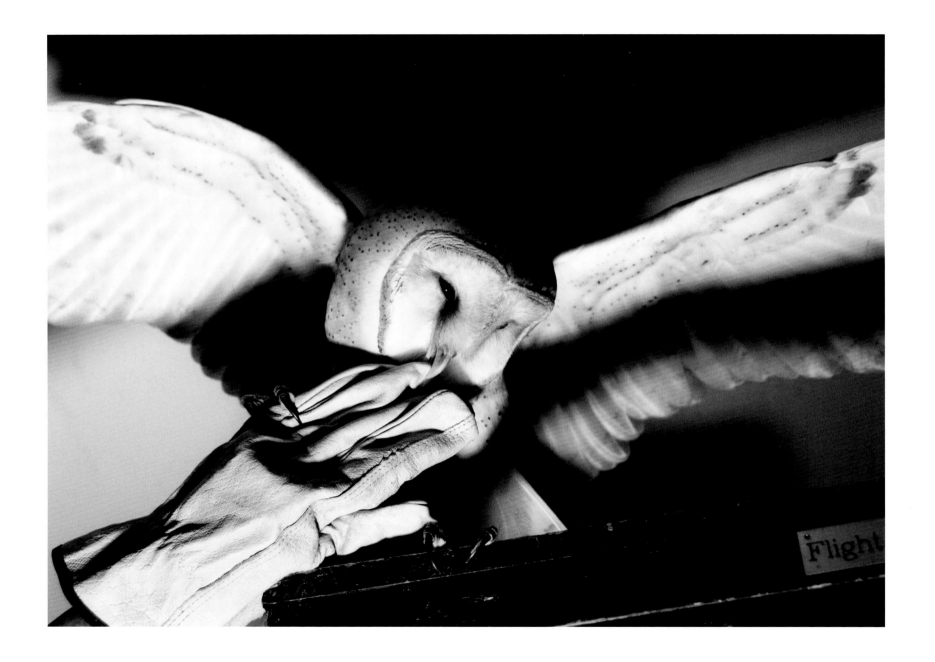

Iya with Kestrel

Iya and Leslie

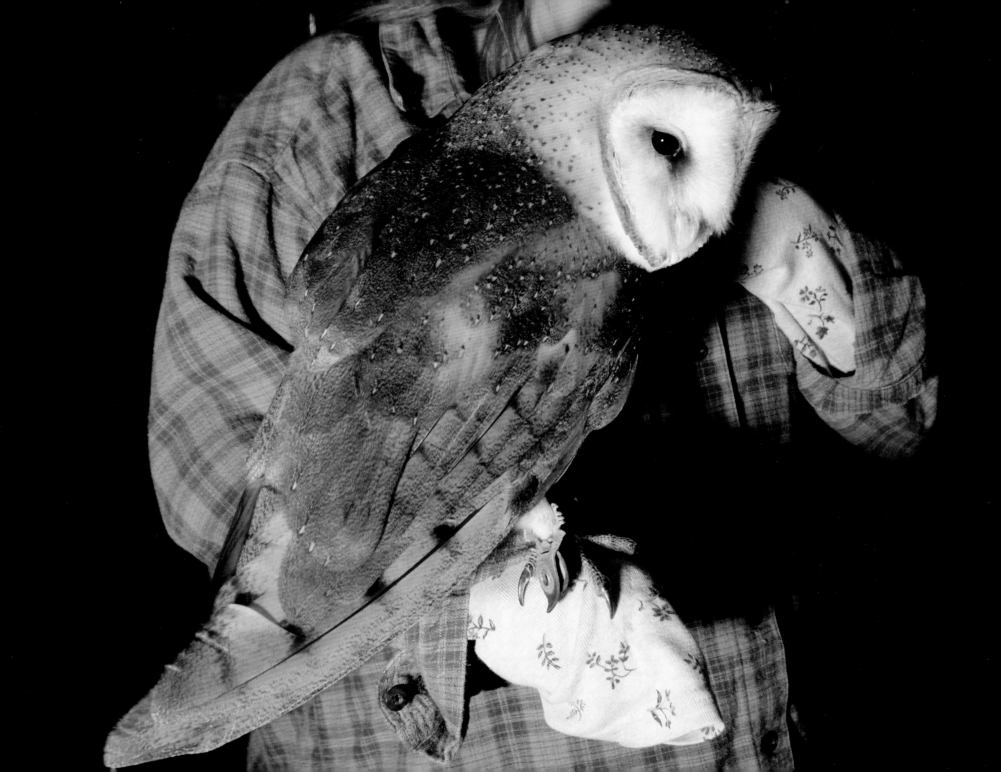

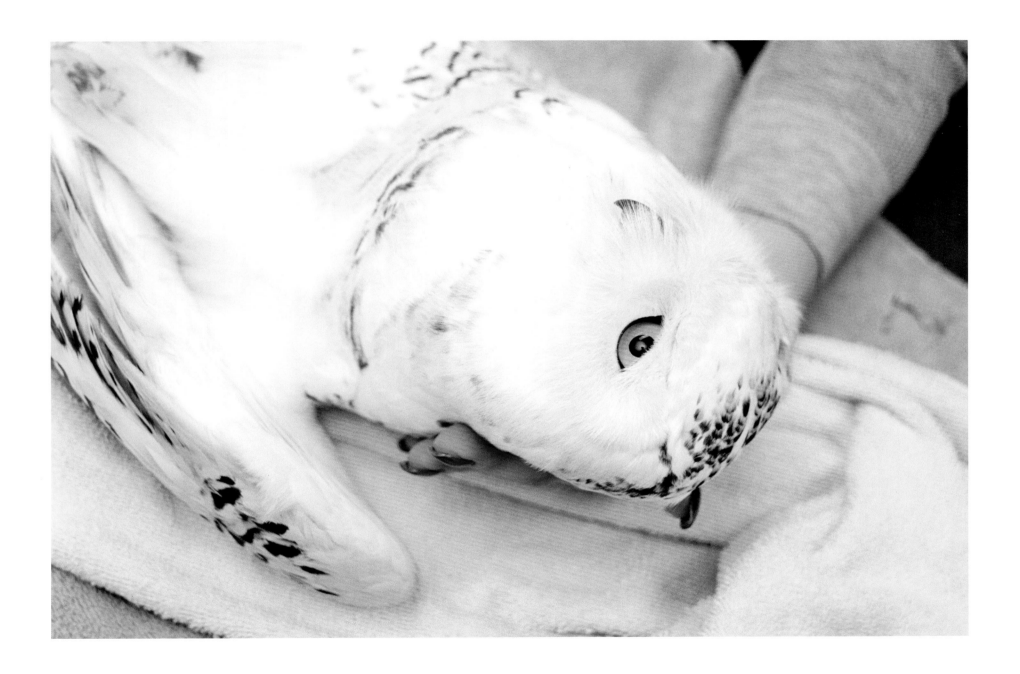

Nanjiska's First Day at Sarvey

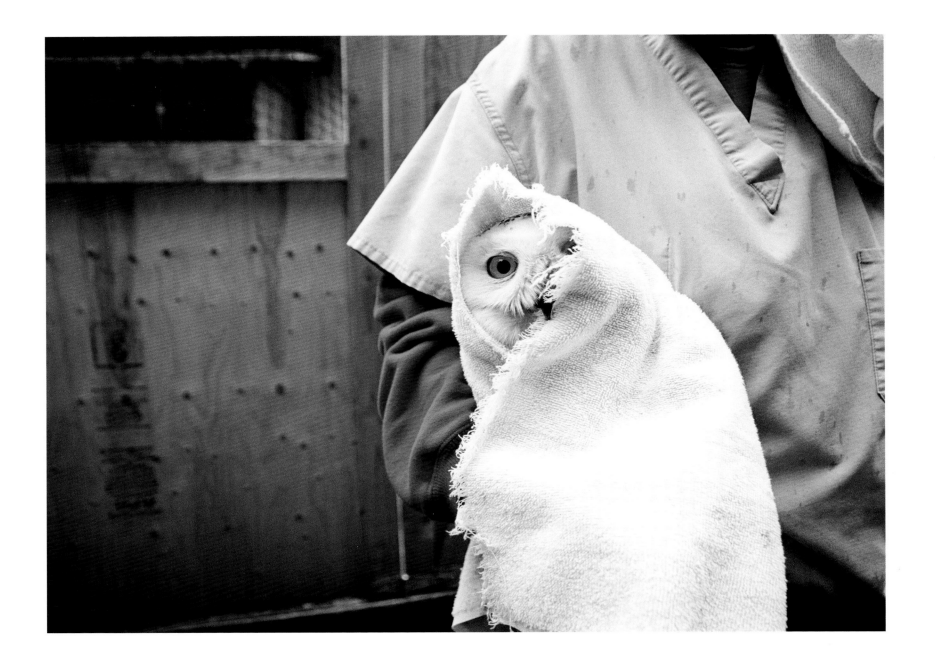

Nanjiska Going to Her Outdoor Enclosure

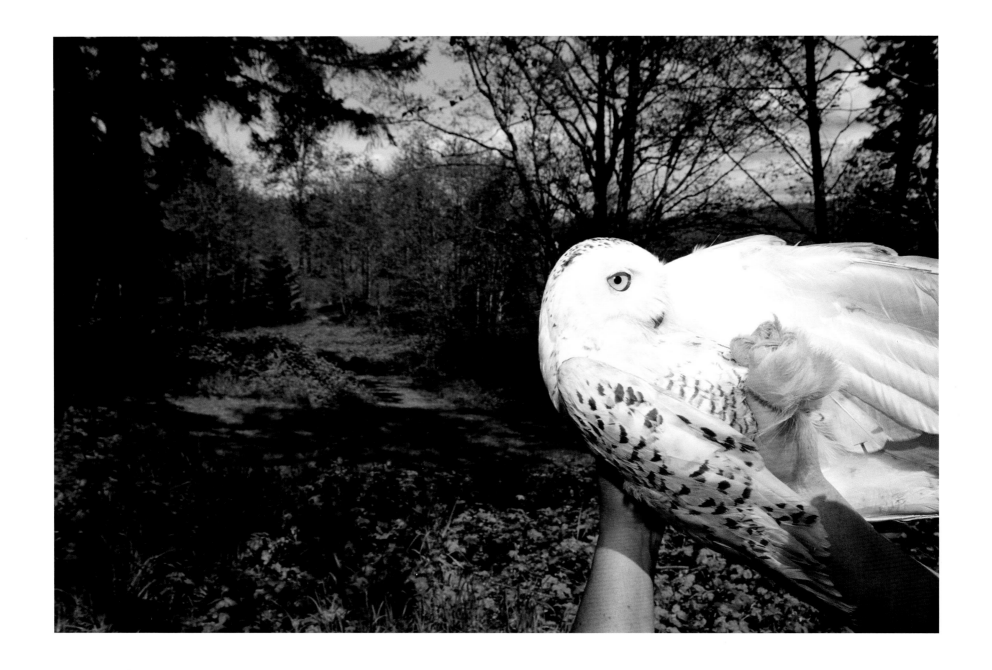

Nanjiska Will Not Fly Again

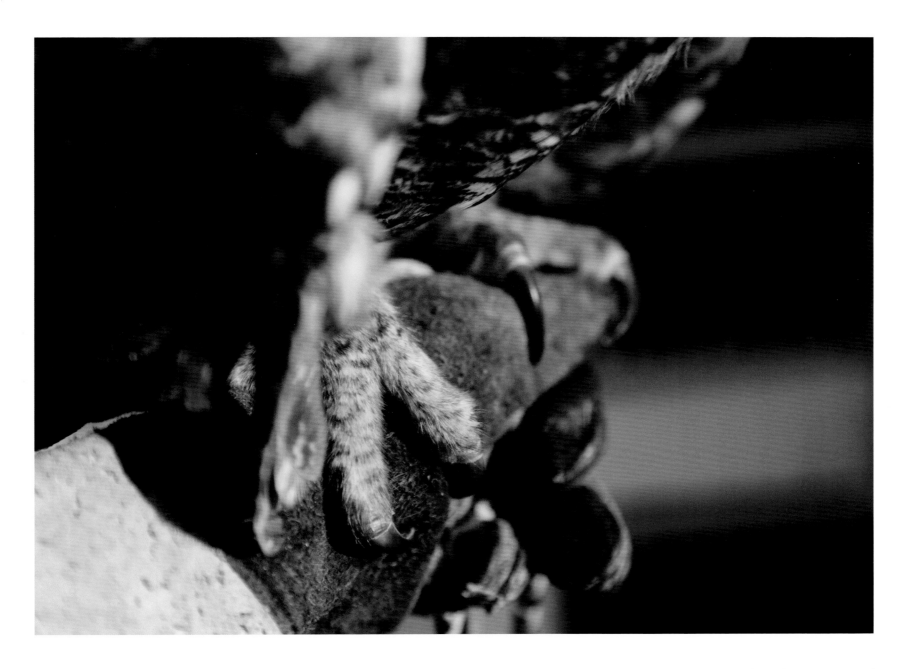

Great Horned Owl Talons Detail
right: Great Horned Owl on the Med Room Table

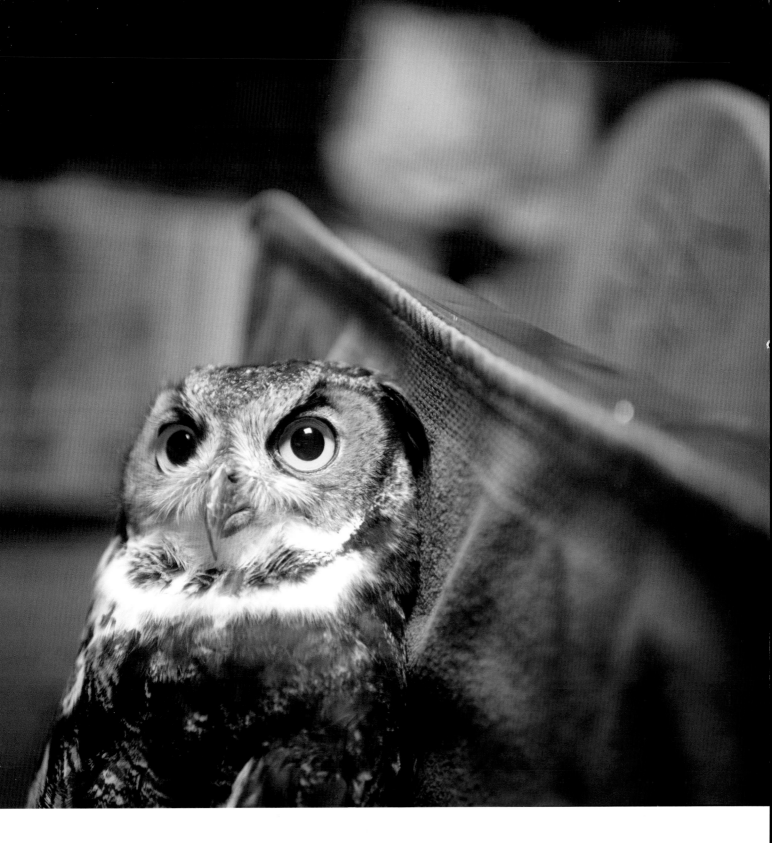

Net for Catching Birds

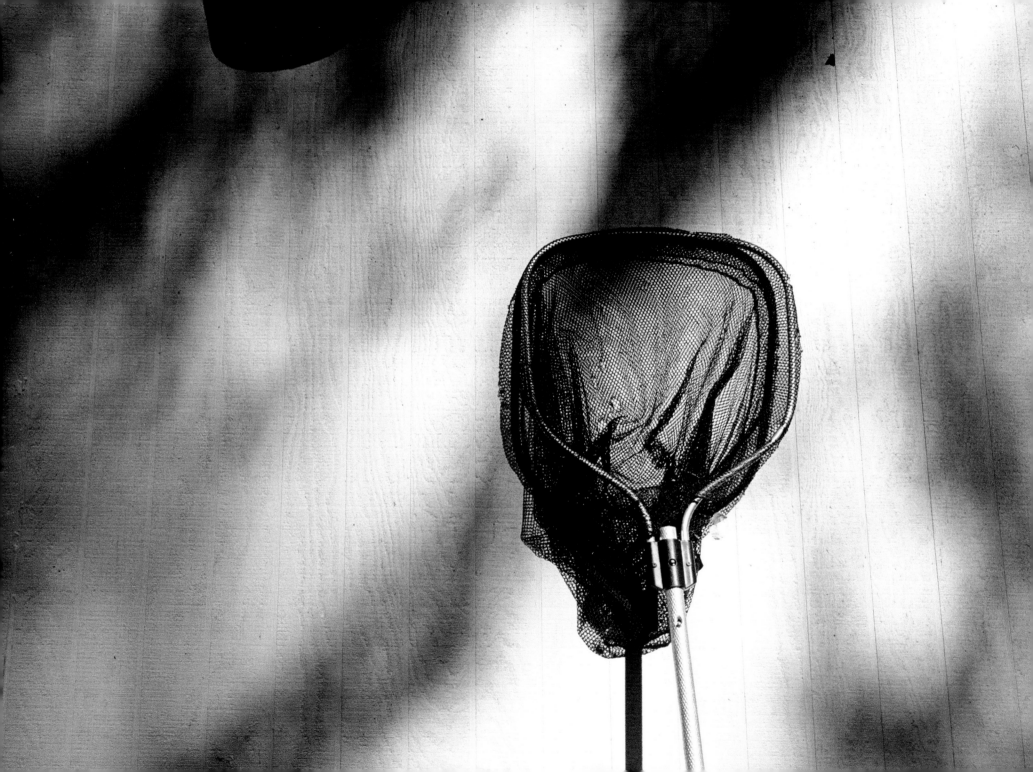

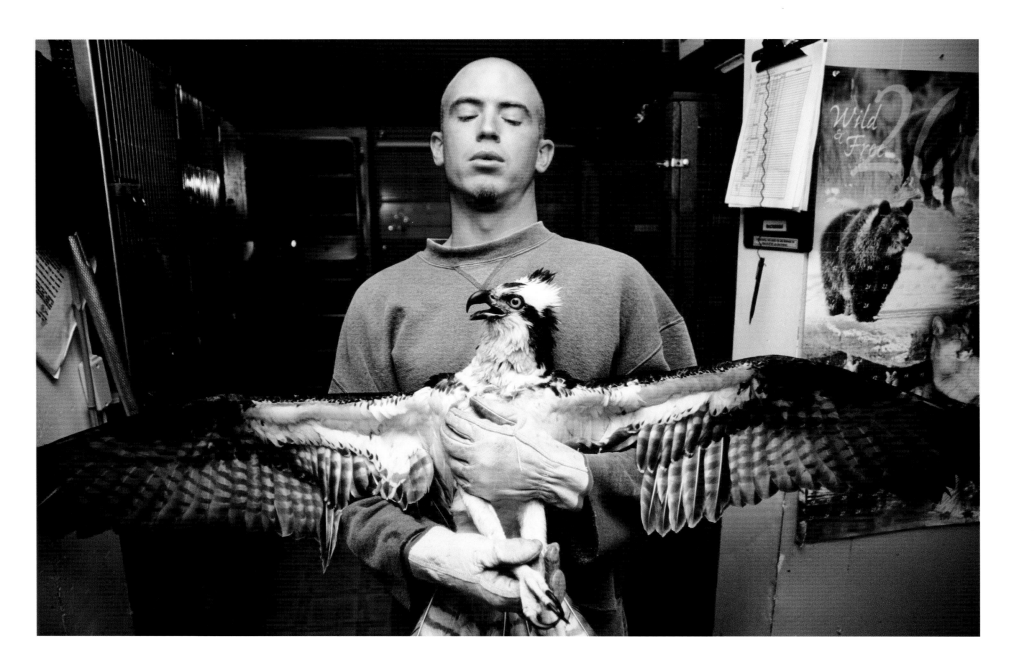

Noel with an Osprey

Eagle in the Med Room

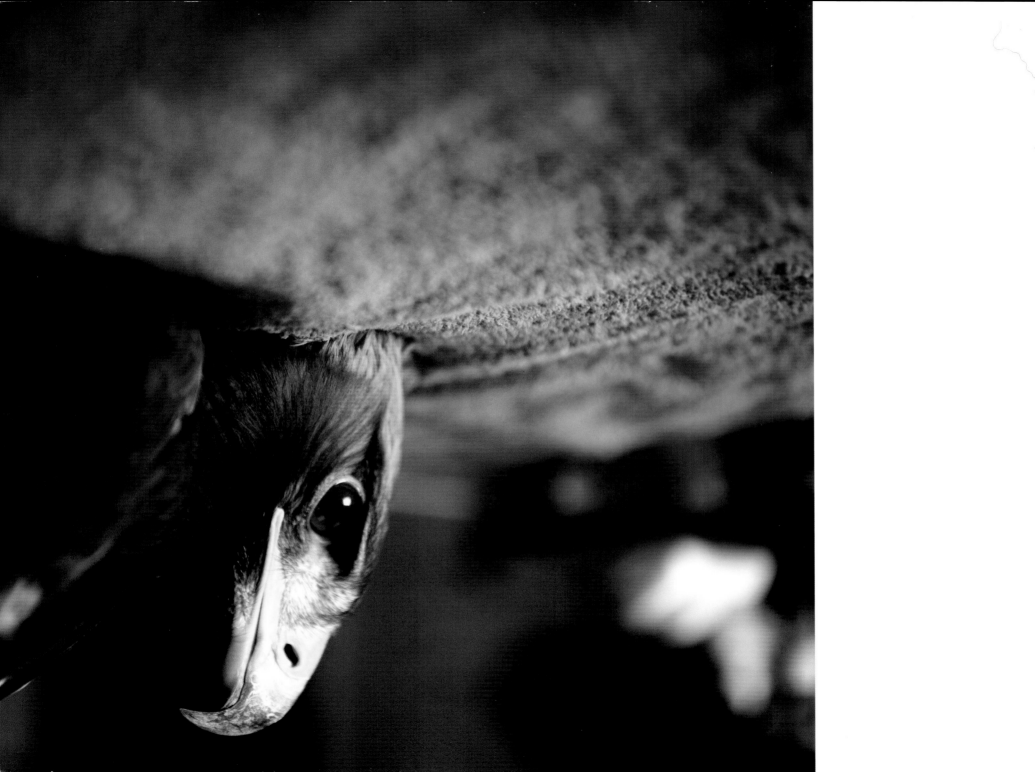

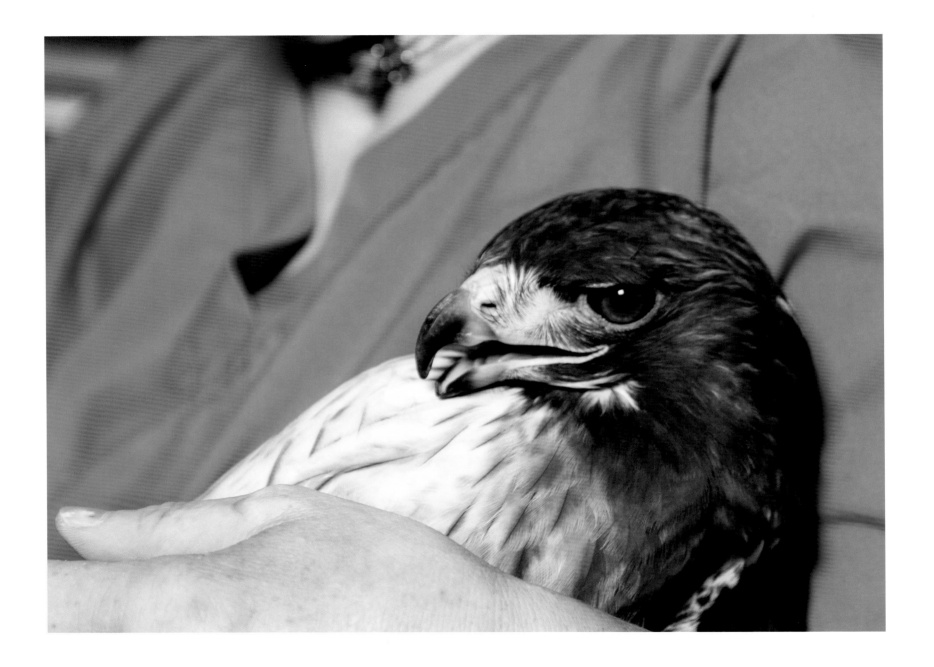

Red-Tailed Hawk with Kestrel

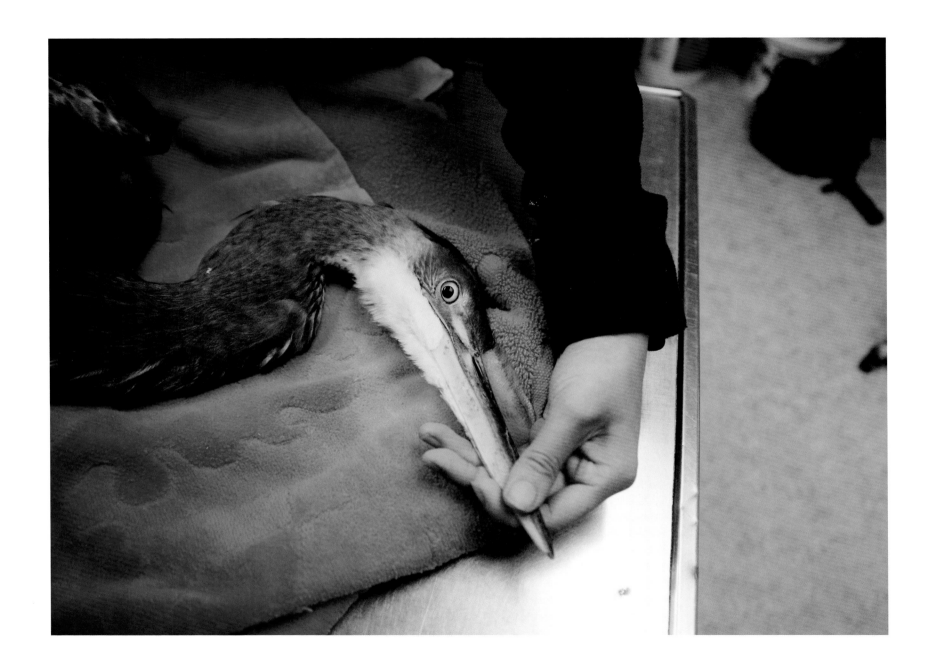

Great Blue Heron on the Med Room Table

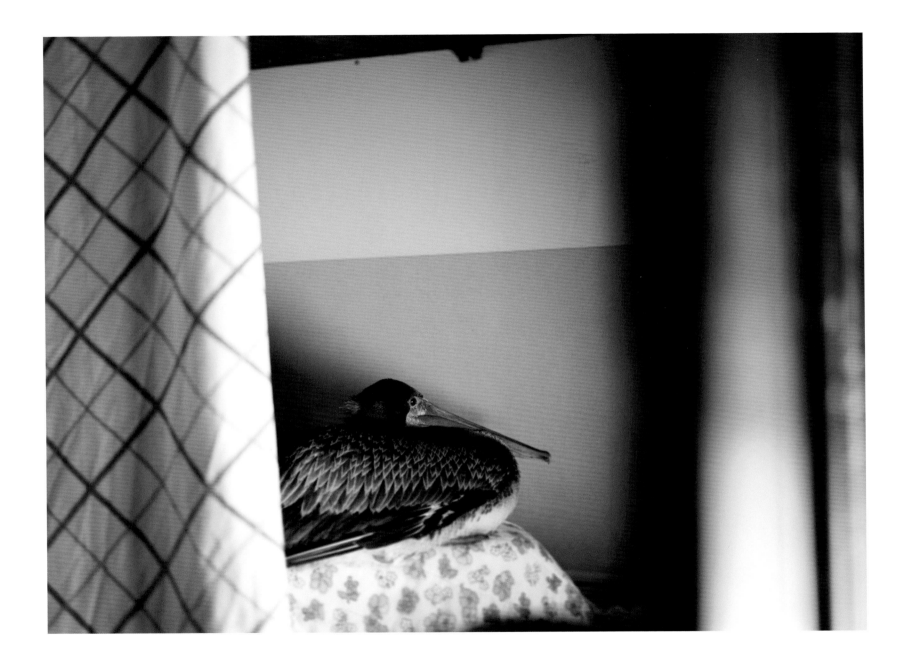

Pelican in Her Cage

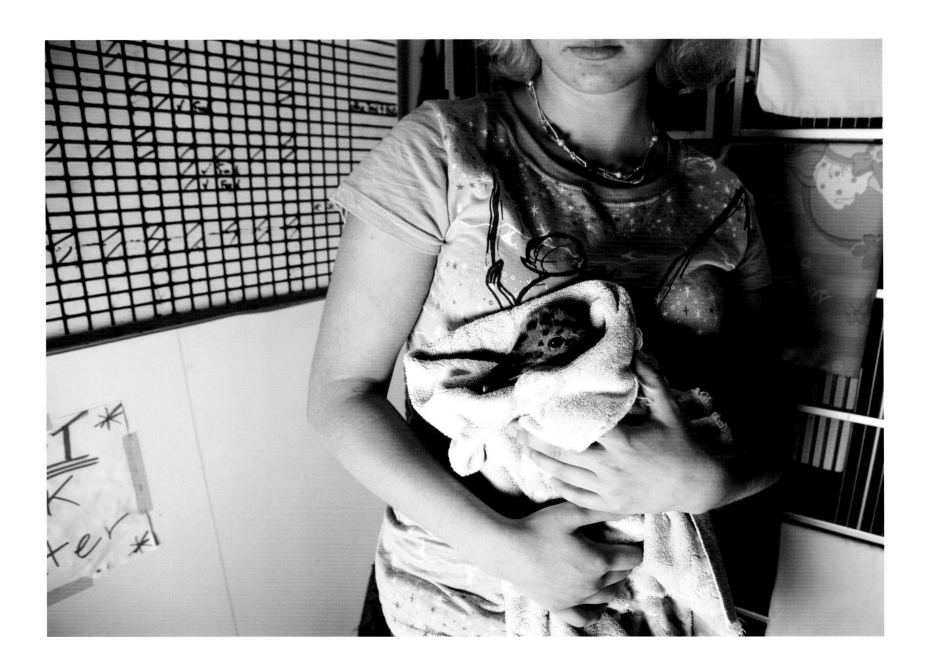

Juvenile Glaucous Winged Gull with Nikki

Juvenile Nighthawk

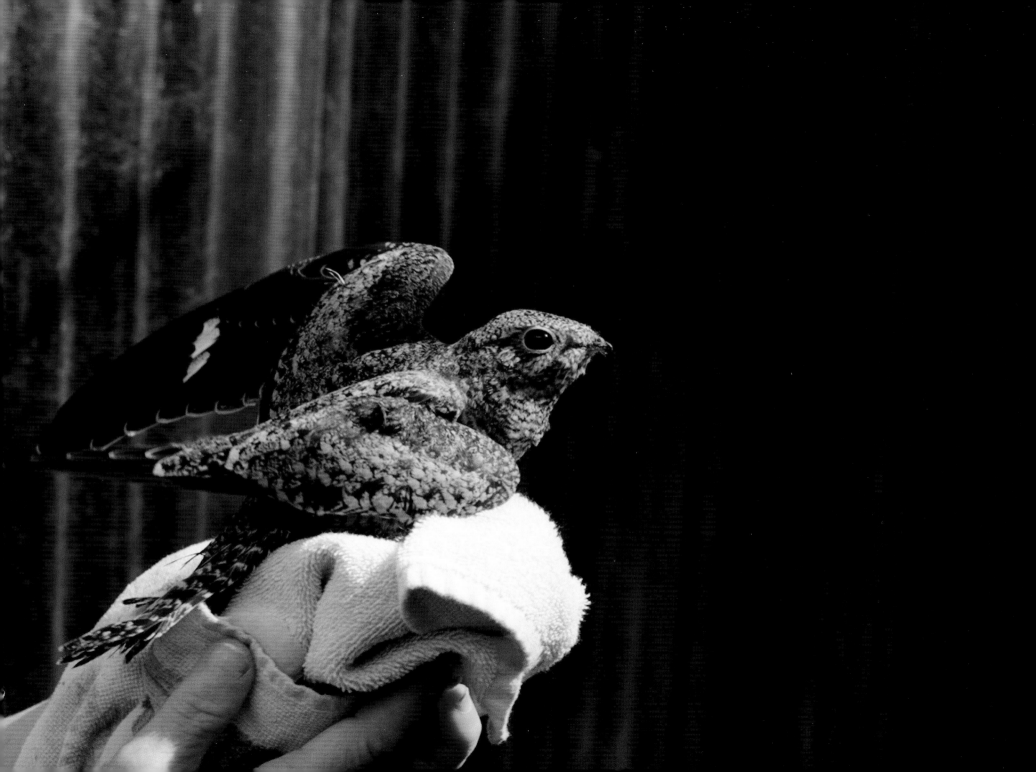

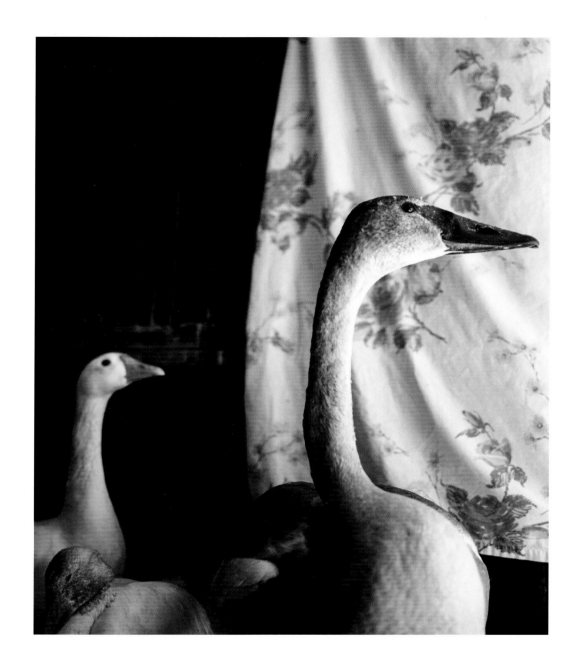

Trumpeter Swan with Friends

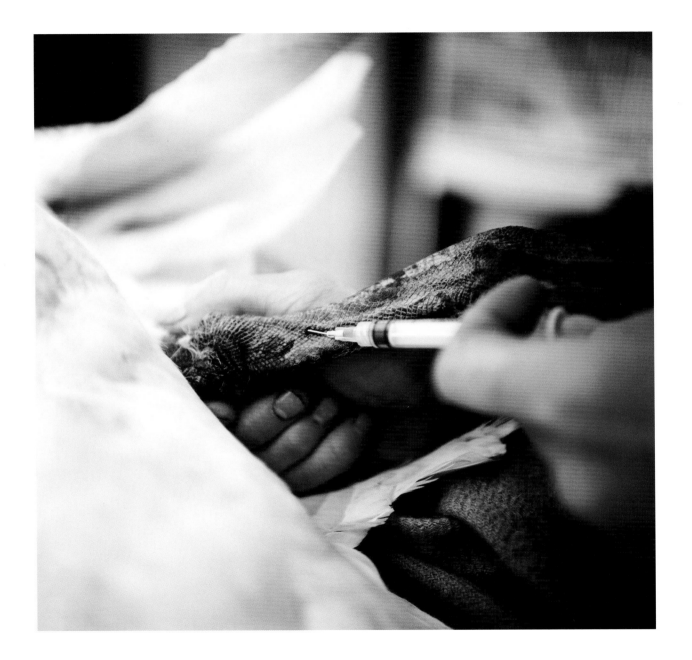

Trumpeter Swan Receiving Medication

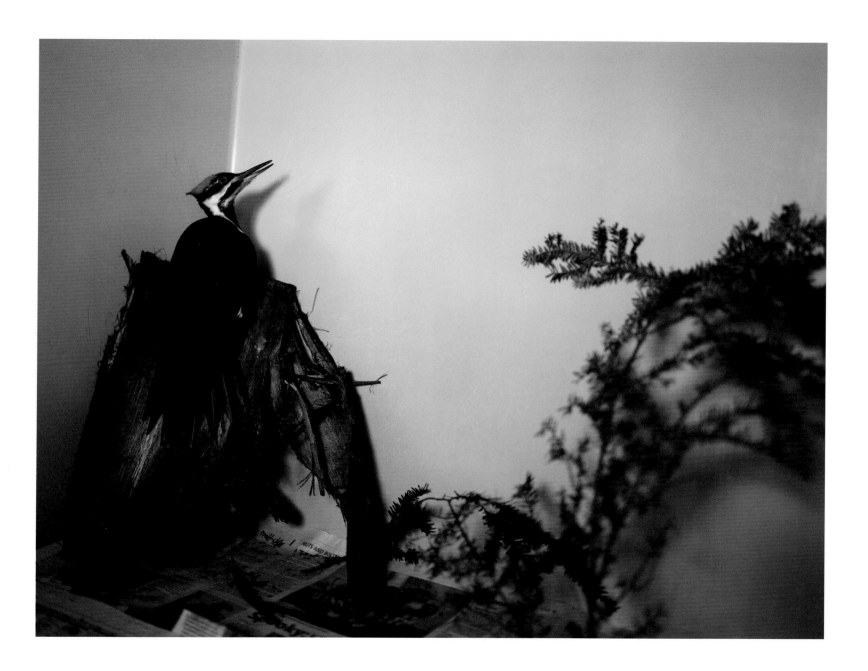

Woodpecker
right: Woodpecker in Suzy's Sweatshirt

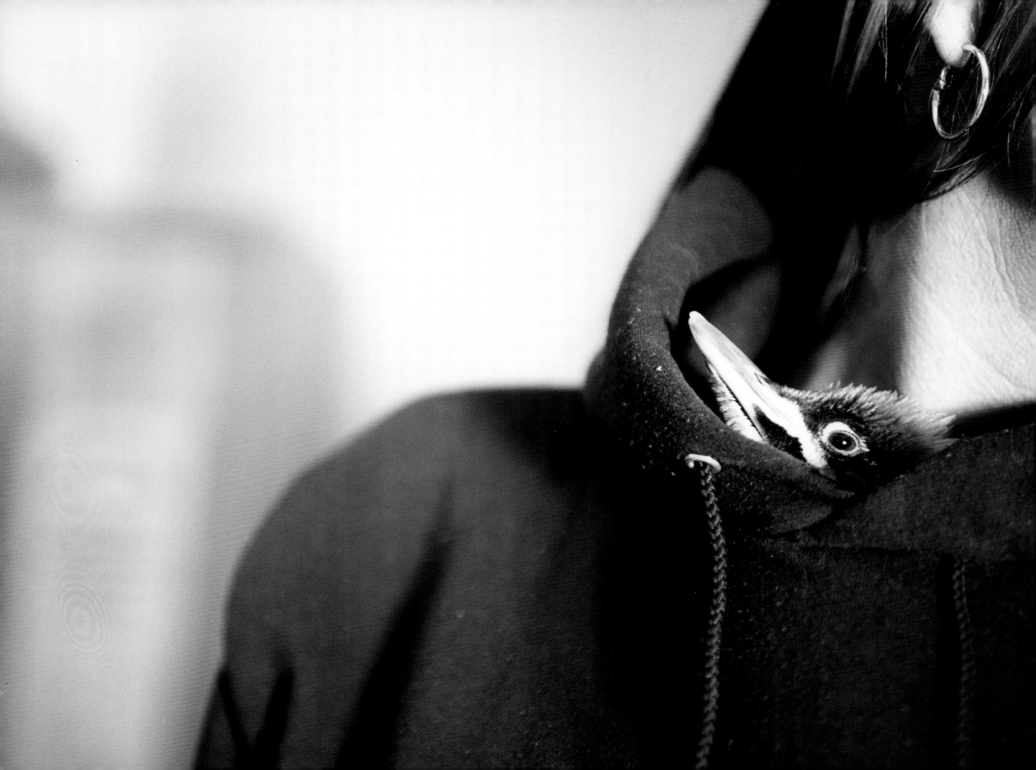

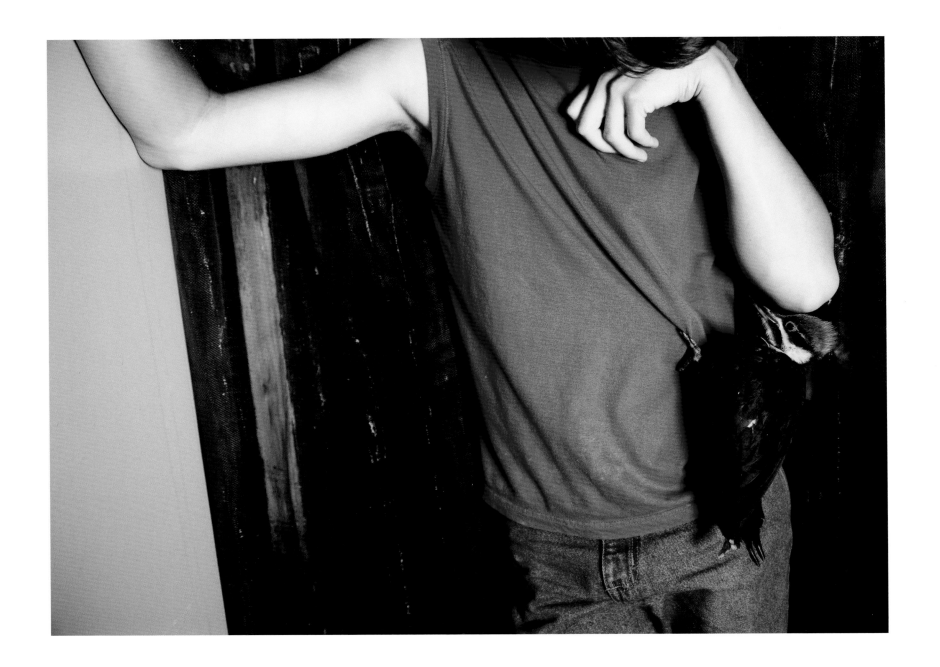

Woodpecker with Daniel

Juvenile Green Heron

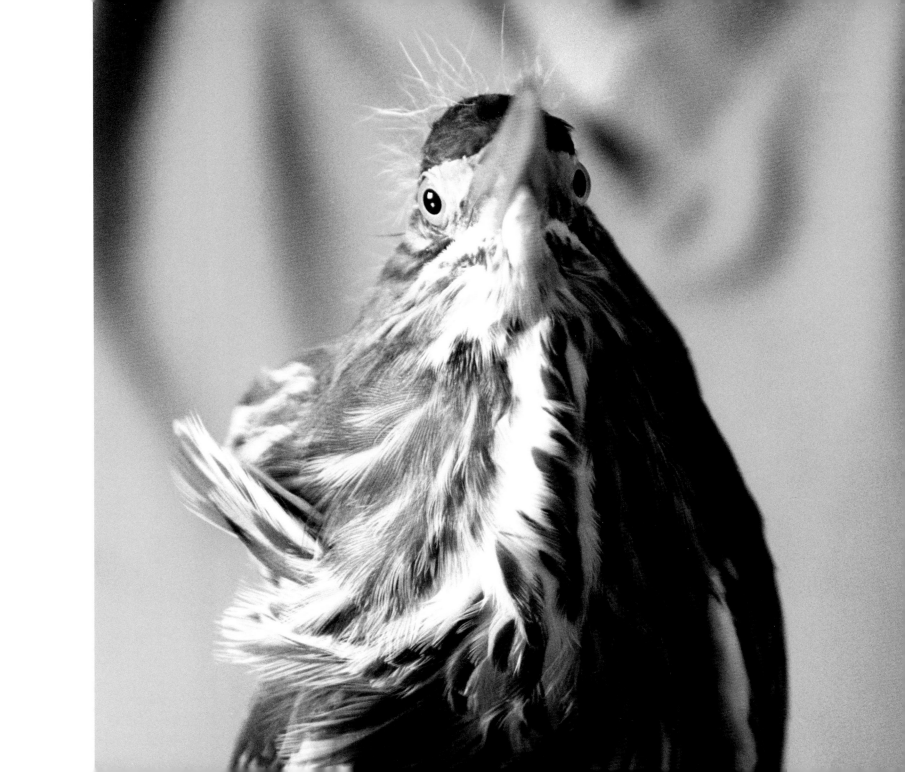

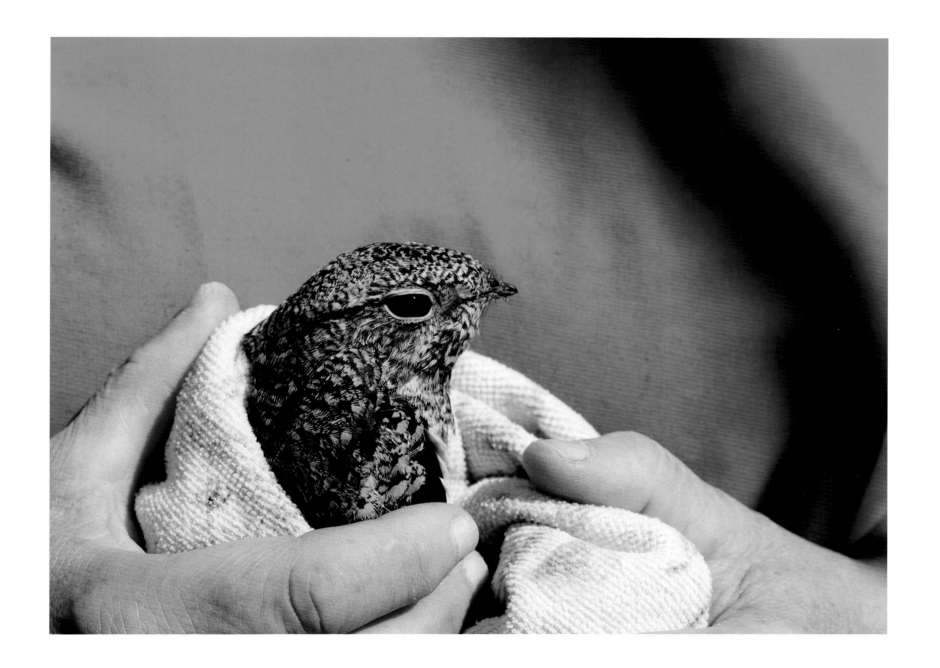

Nighthawk in Blue

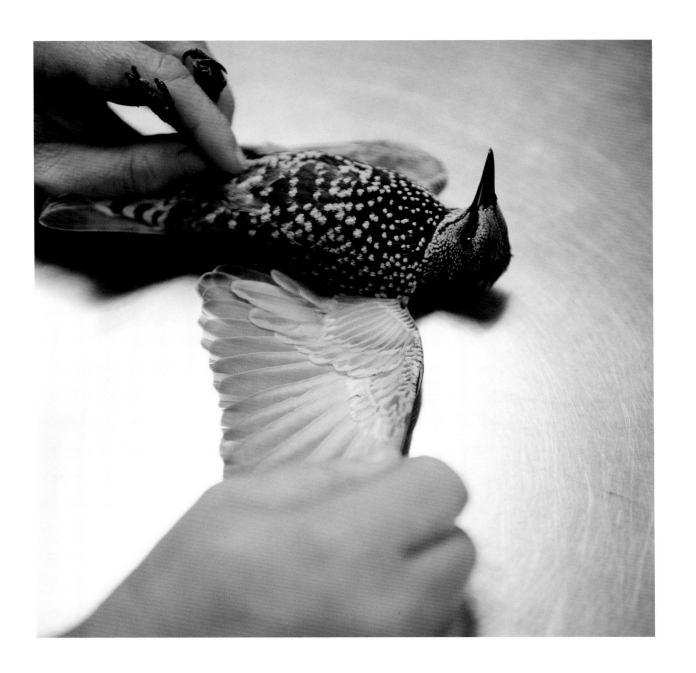

Starling with Wing Damage

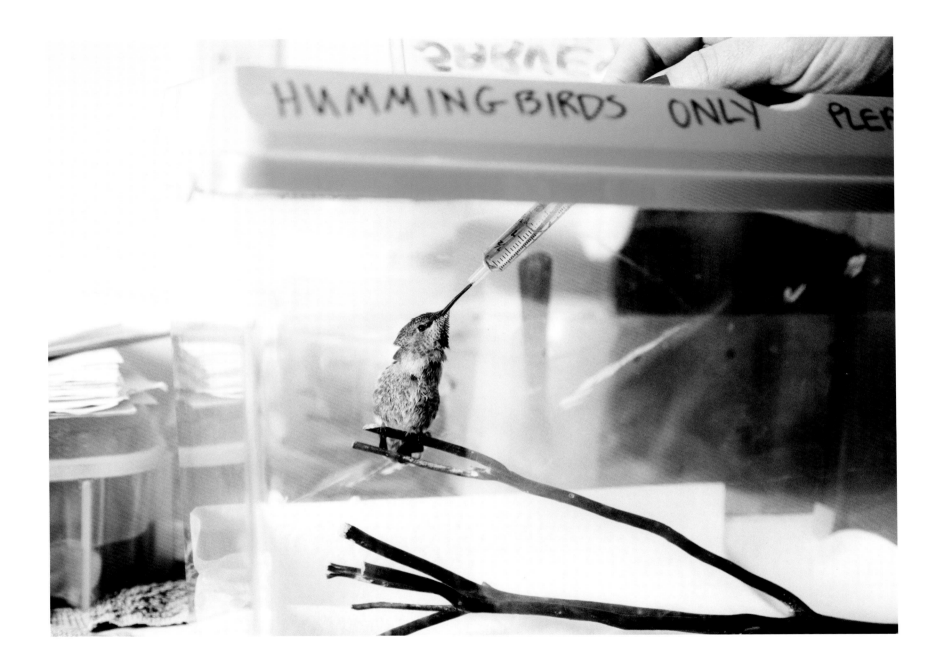

Hummingbird Receiving Fluids

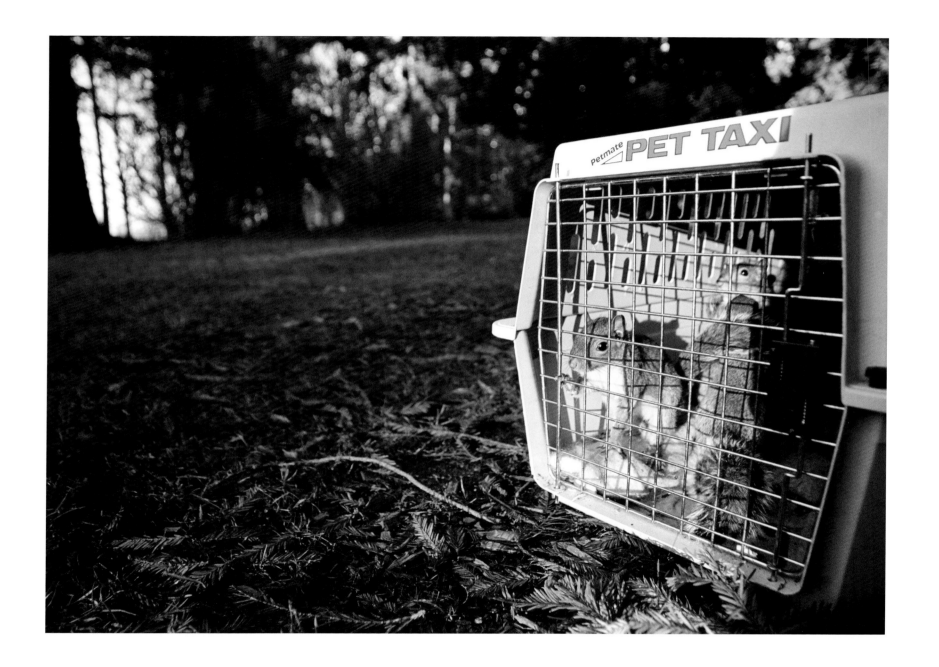

Squirrel Release #1

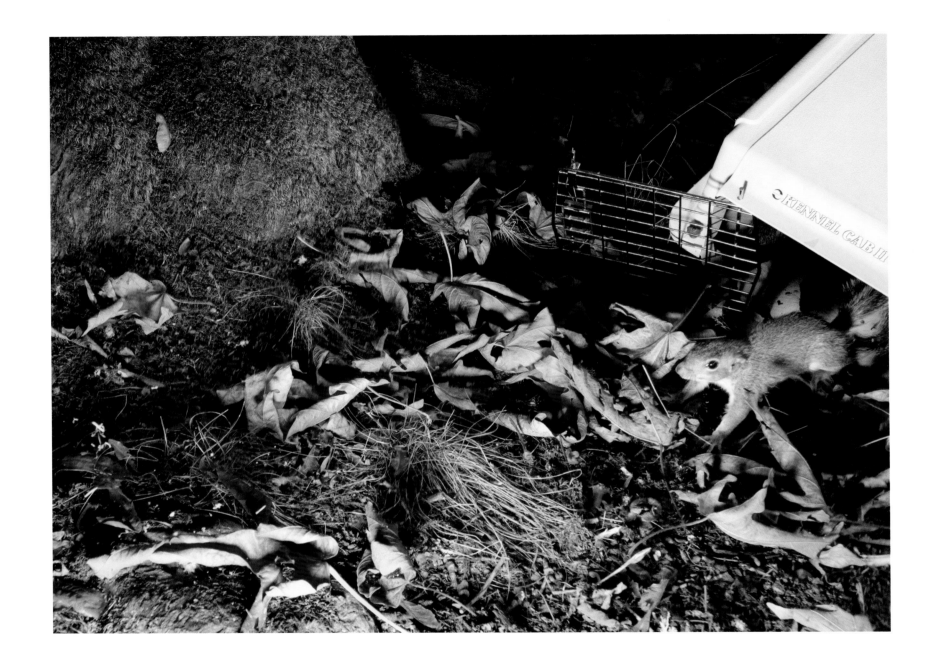

Squirrel Release #2

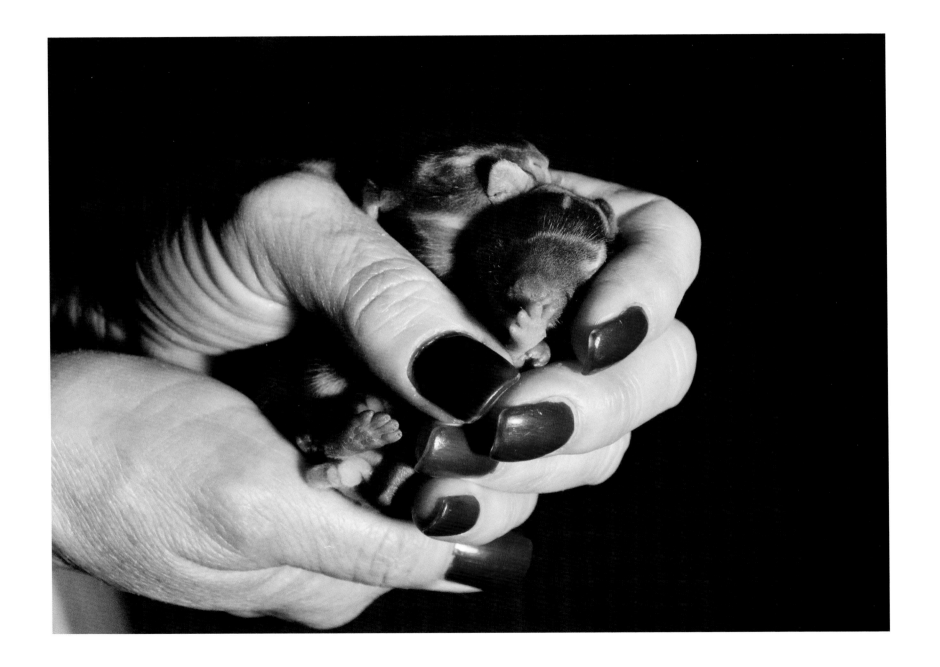

Cottontail Rabbits in Suzy's Hands

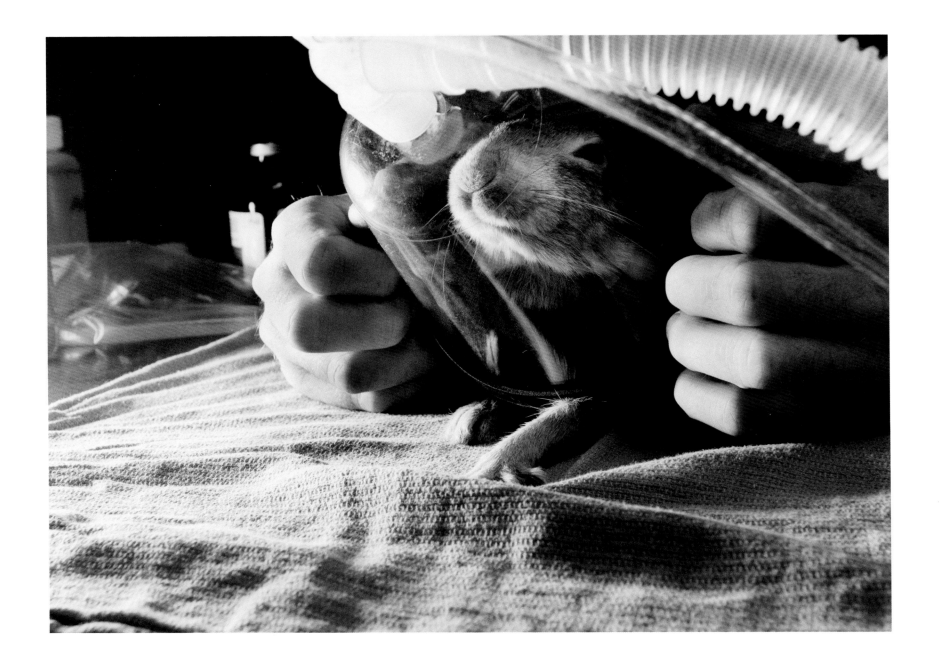

Cottontail Going to Heaven

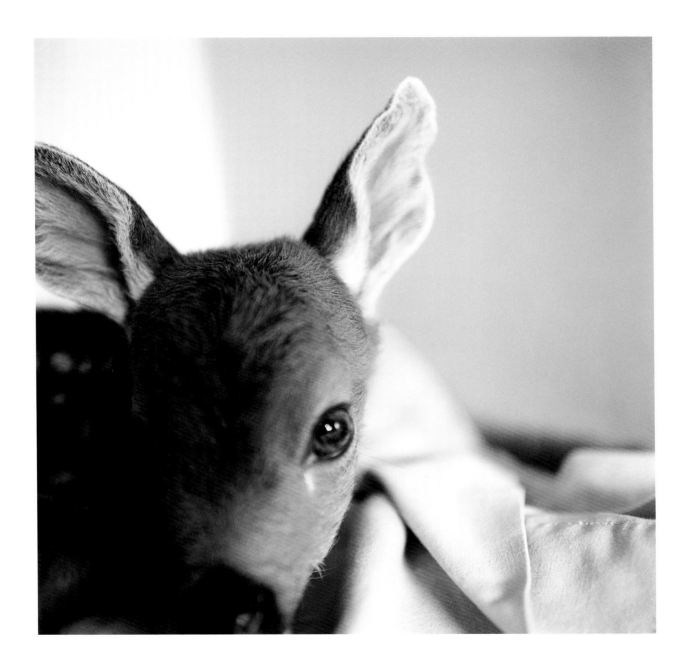

Fawn with Blue Eyes

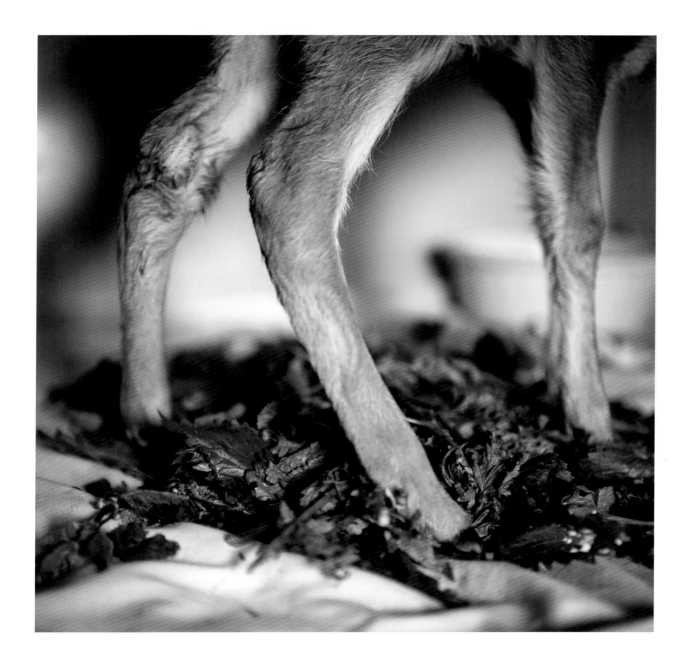

Fawn Legs with Blackberry Leaves

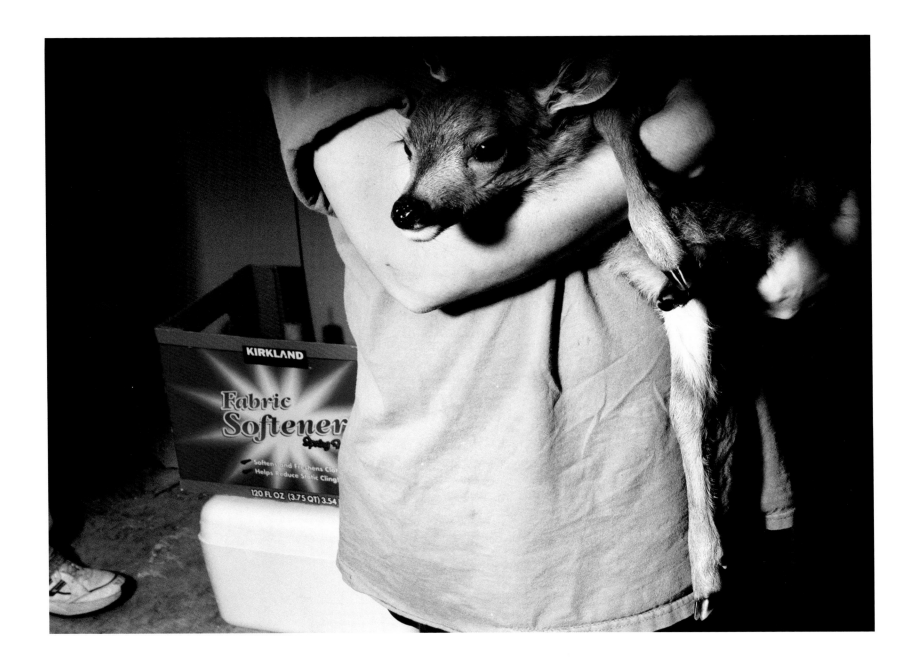

Juvenile Fawn Rescue

Fawn Looking into Spring

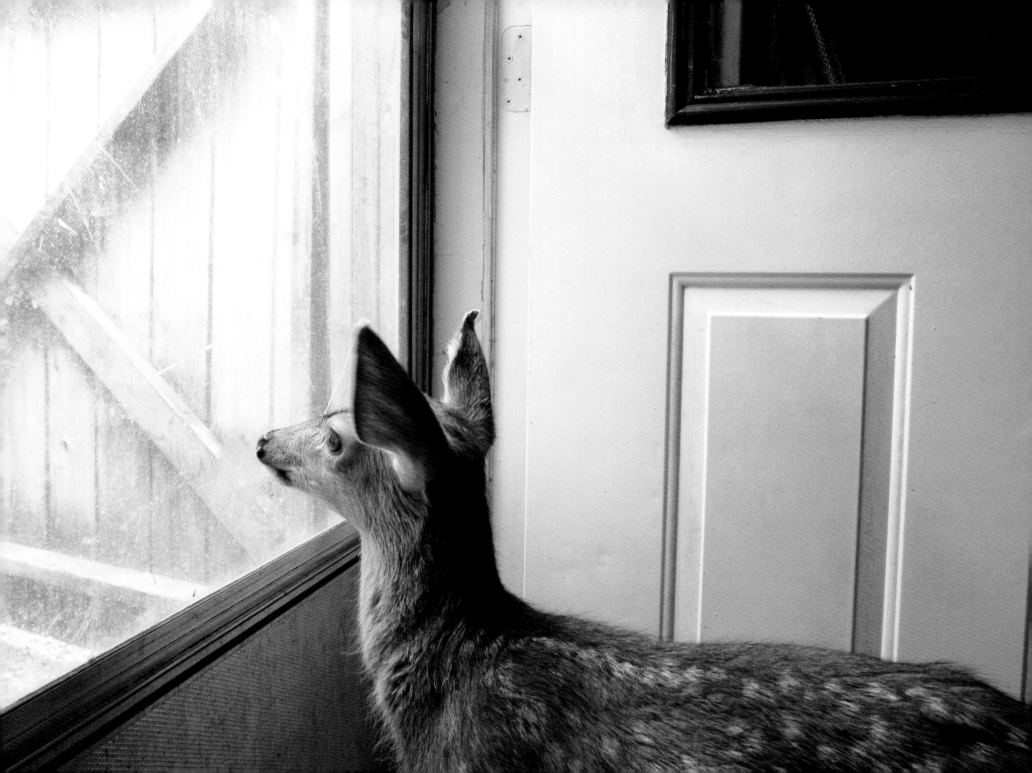

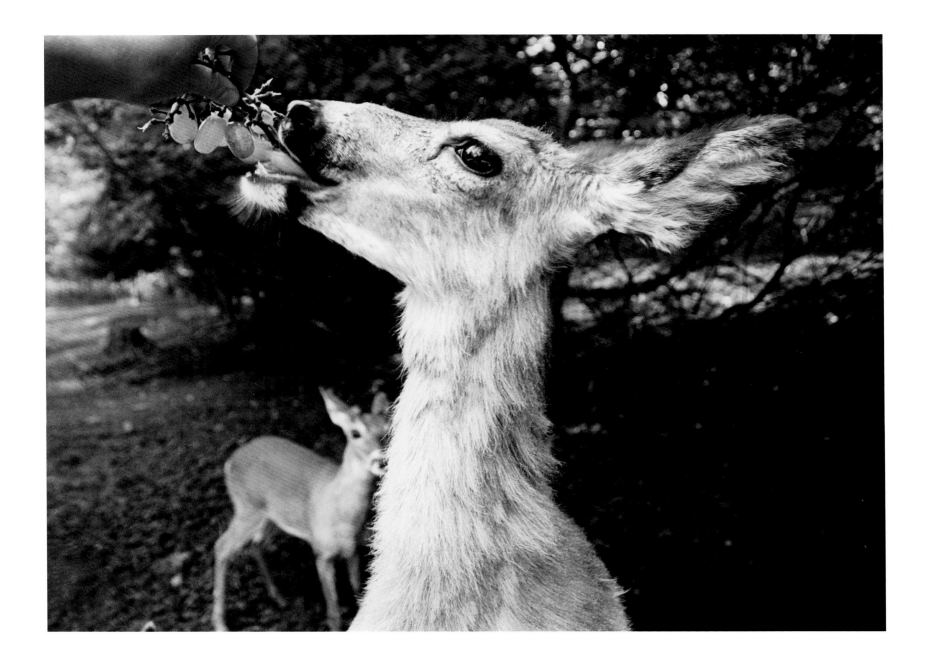

Deer with Grapes

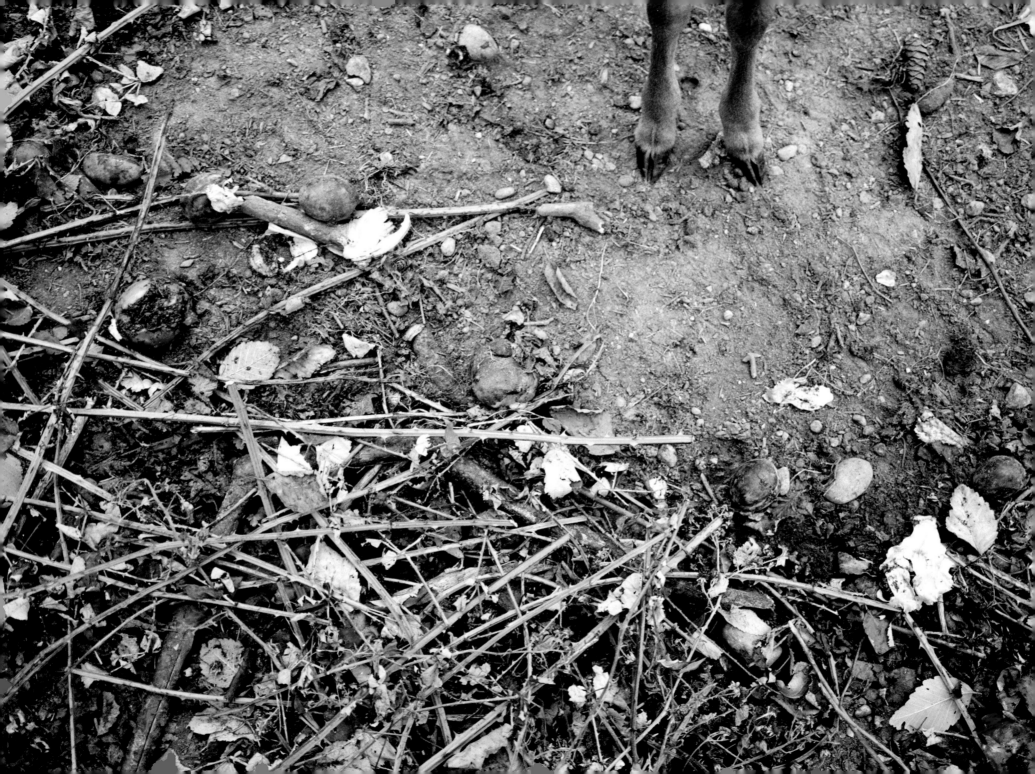

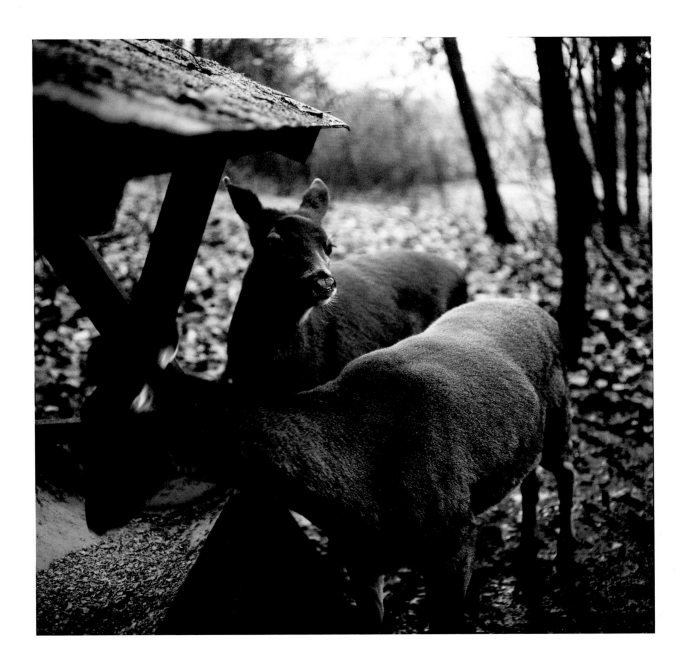

Two Deer Eating Breakfast
left: Deer Hooves with Apples and Plums

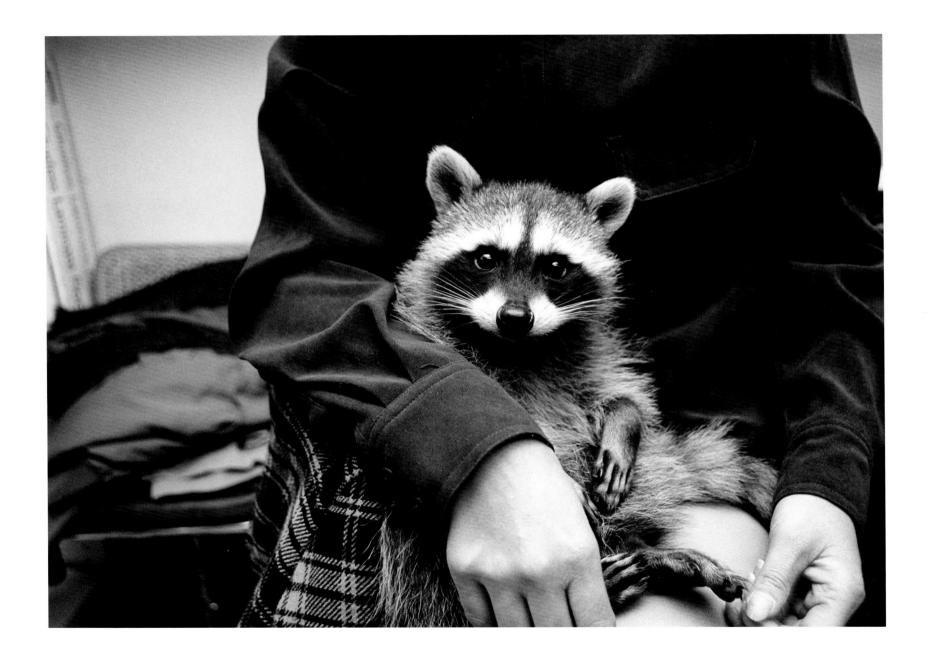

Raccoon Sitting on Robert's Lap with My Coat

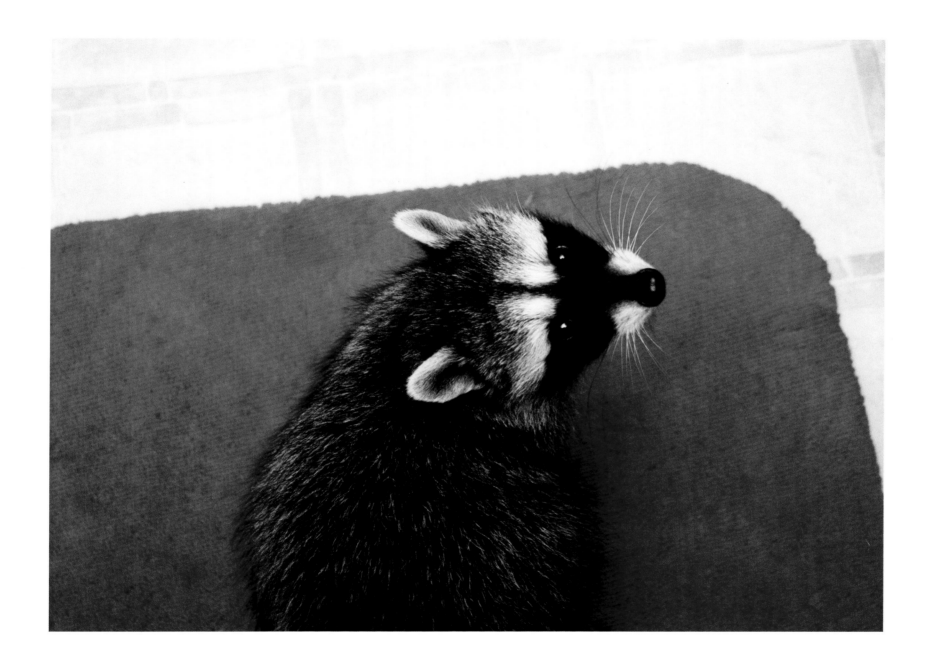

Raccoon on a Red Rug

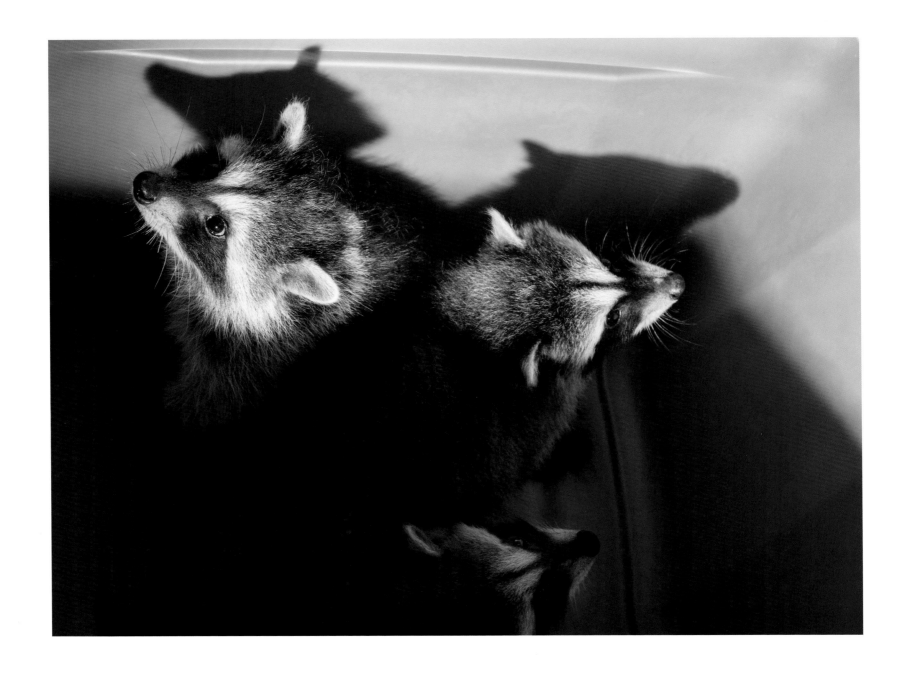

Raccoons Waiting for Their Cage to Be Cleaned

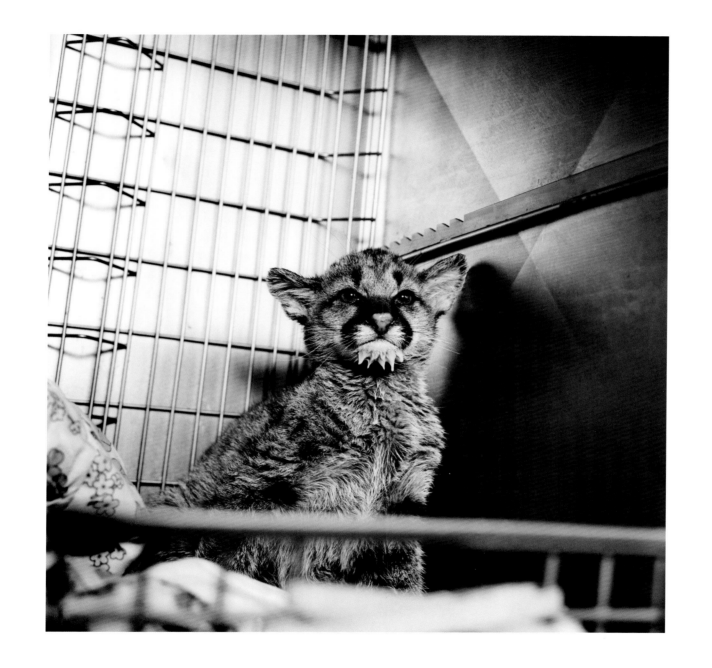

Juvenile Cougar

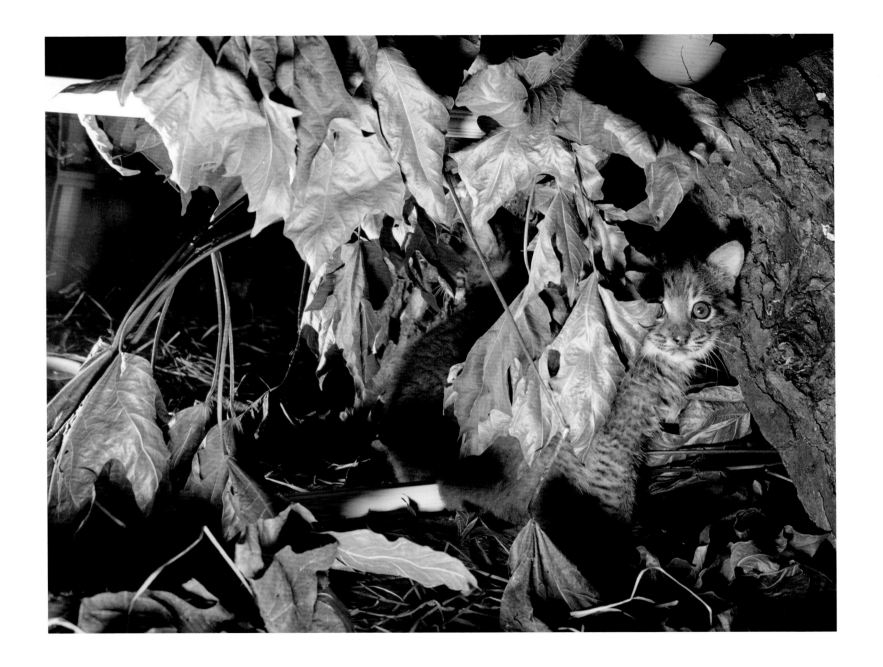

Baby Bobcat with Mirror

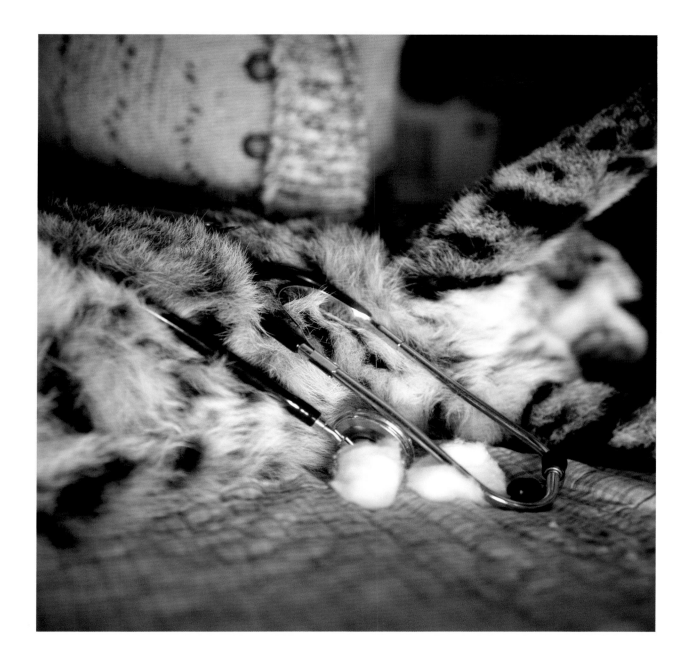

Bobcat Undergoing Surgery

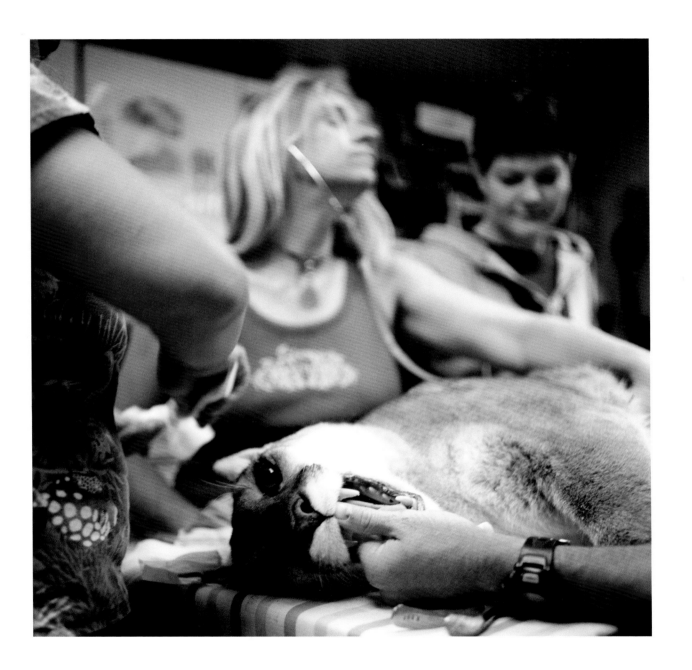

Sasha in the Medroom

Juvenile Coyote

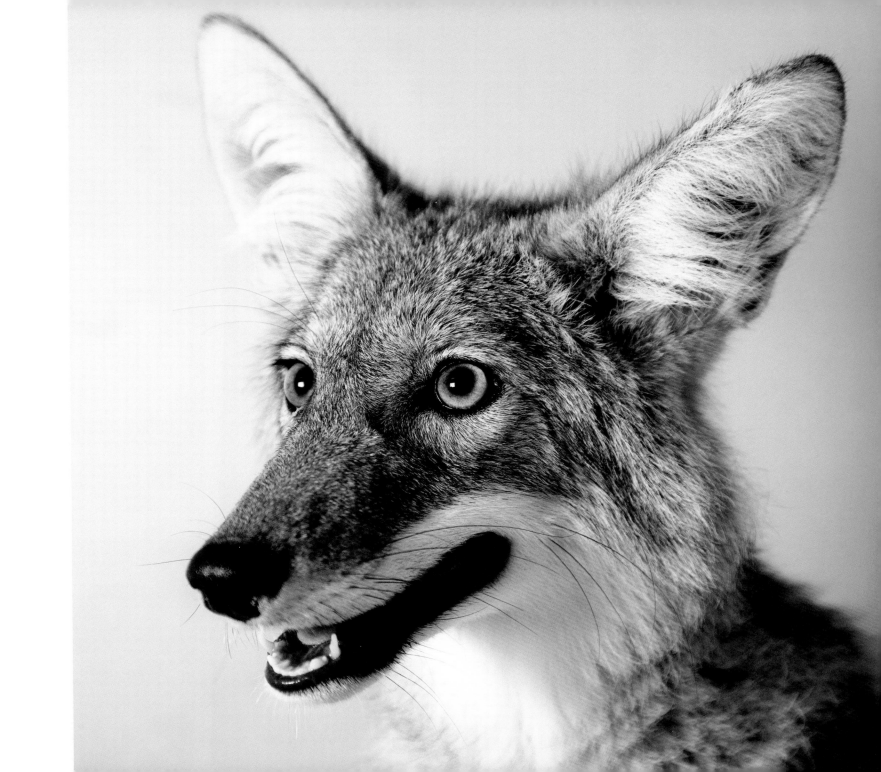

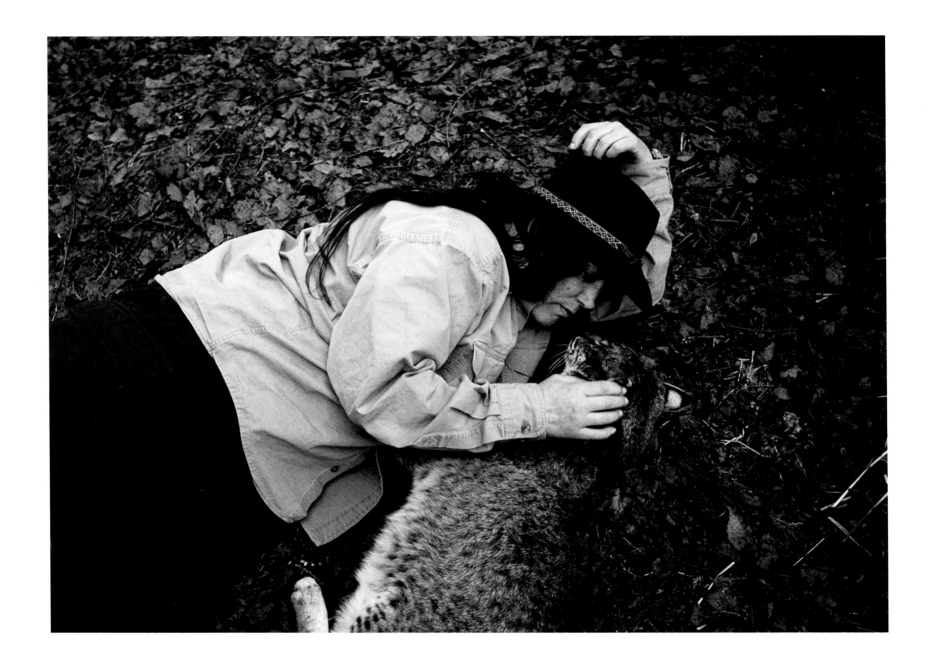

Kestrel with Bear the Bobcat

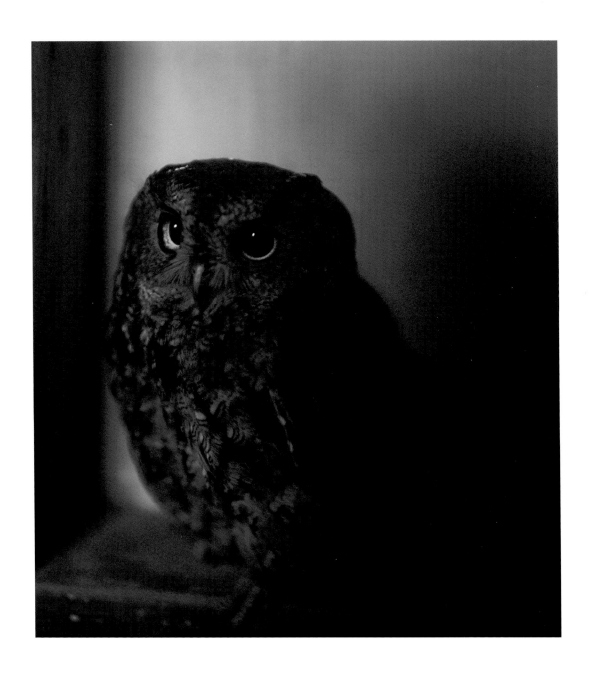

Rafter, Screech Owl

Angel in the Summer

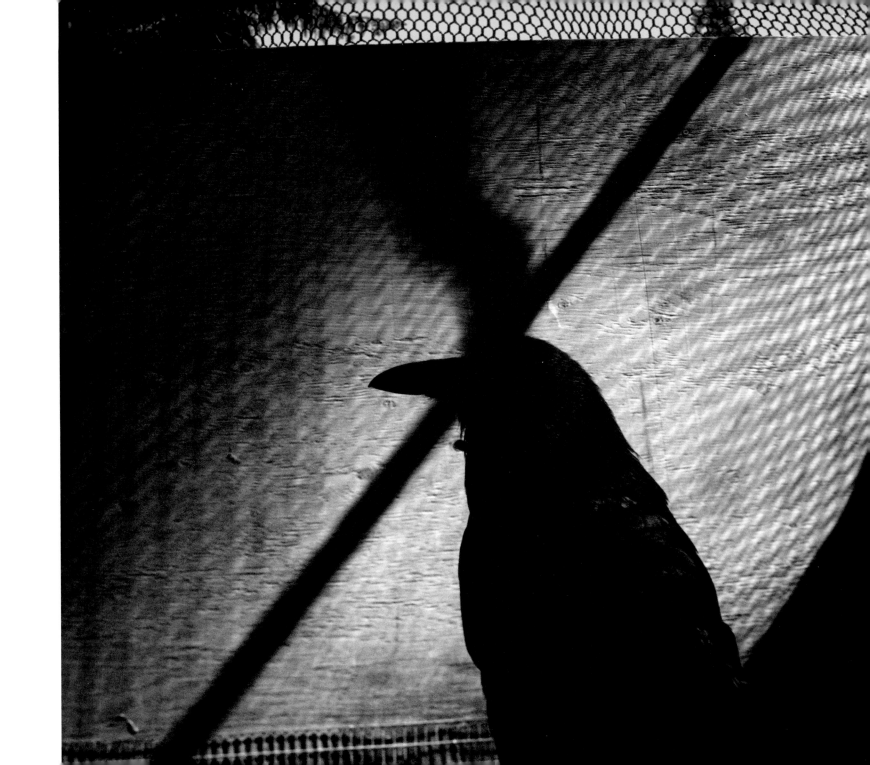

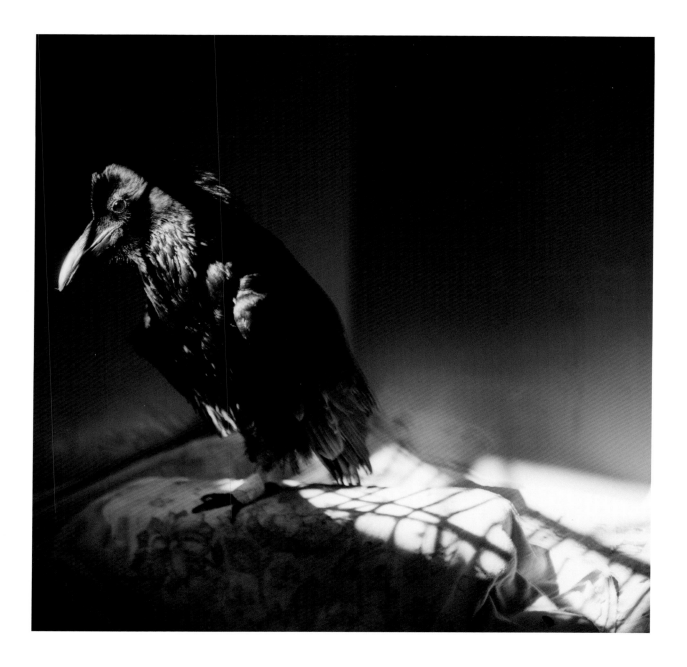

Angel in the Shadows
right: Angel after Surgery

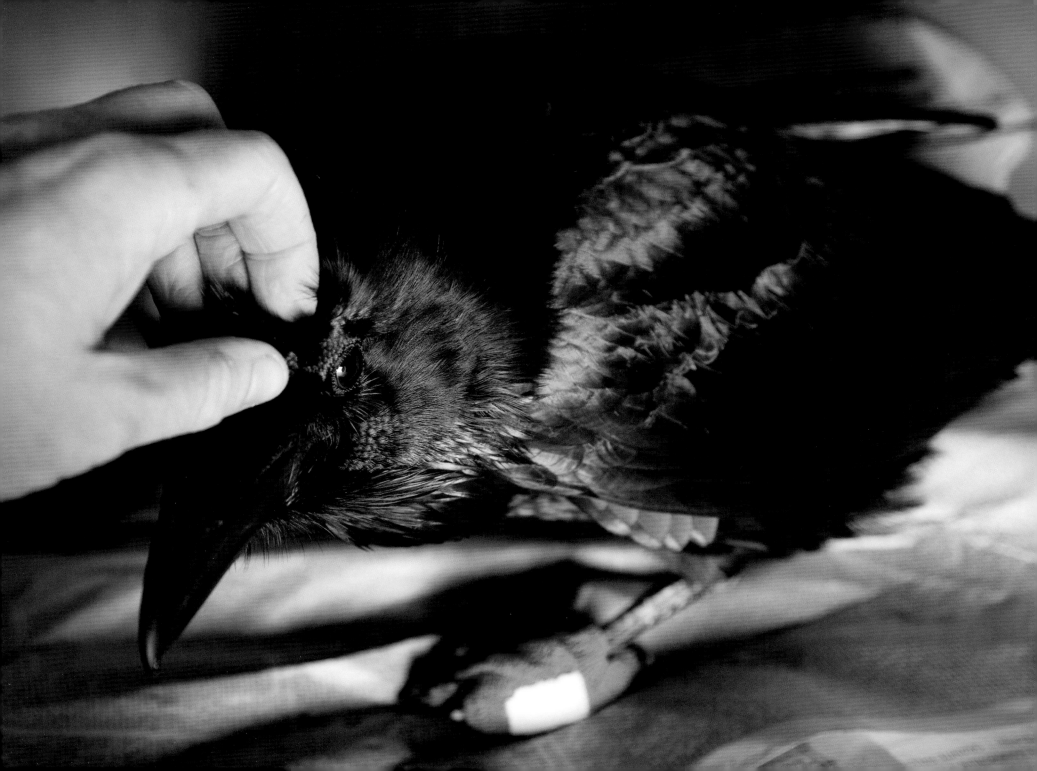

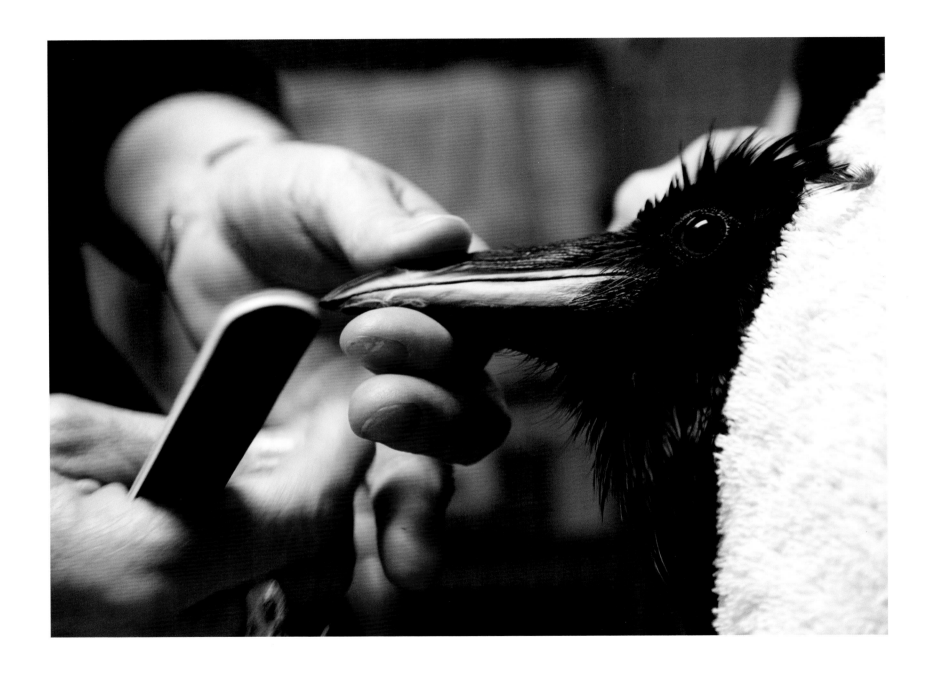

Angel Having Her Beak Trimmed

Angel Undergoing Surgery for Bumble Foot

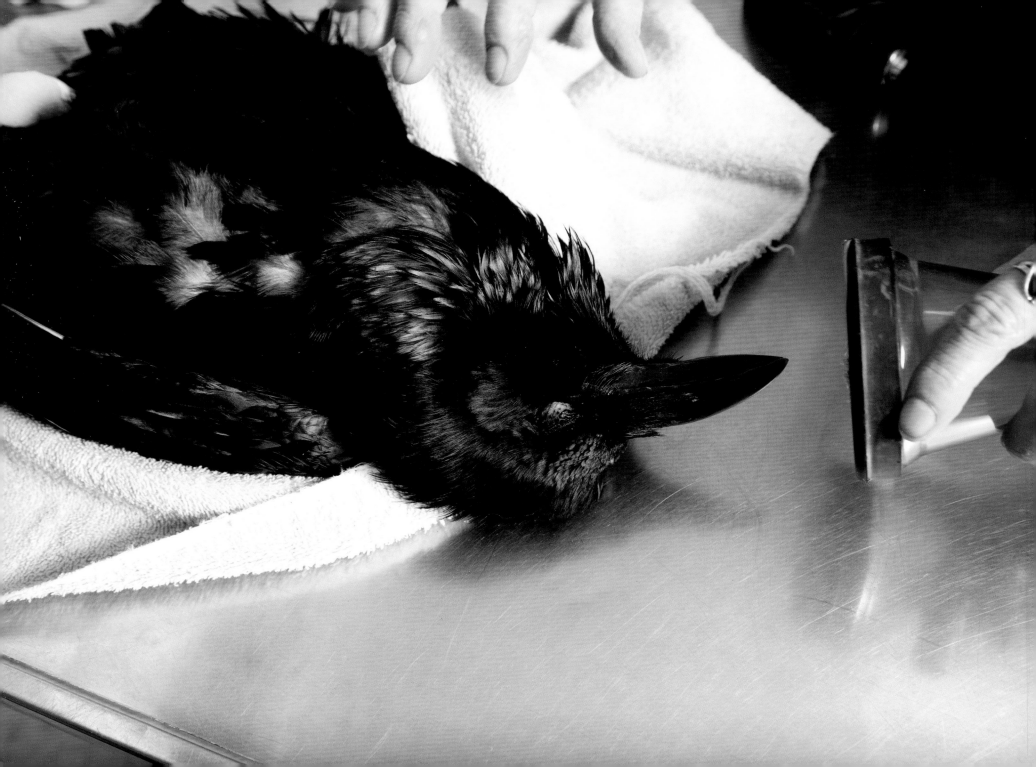

FINDING ANGEL

I was born into a family of animal lovers. My family always had animals at home – usually two cats and, a dog and sometimes a new creature would join us. I was in 4-H; my sister rescued stray cats and dogs; my mom worked for a veterinary clinic; my dad would gently pick up spiders and escort them out the door to safety. We all believed in giving everything the greatest chance of survival. A city girl, I dreamed of having horses and pigs and sleeping alongside them in their stables.

Years later in my adult life, I found a small, sick pigeon wobbling around in Seattle. After calling 911 I received a call from the Sarvey Wildlife Care Center (50 miles from Seattle), and the man on the other line said he'd be here in an hour. My husband and I waited with the pigeon, and as soon as the Sarvey help arrived, I asked if the Center needed any volunteers. »Are you kidding?« I took that as an emphatic »Yes«.

My discovery of Sarvey in Arlington, Washington, forever changed my connection to the animal world. Located in the quiet foothills of the lush Cascade Mountain Range, Sarvey is home to coyote runs, duck ponds, deer fields, bear cages, beaver pools, and raptor flights. It is an animal shantytown held together by rare donations and lots of love, and in love I fell.

I prepared for my first visit to Sarvey in the fall of 2003. Longing for a photography project that was personally meaningful and could also be of service, I brought my camera. I had just lost my mother, and Sarvey soon became the place that helped me understand the real meaning of life. I discovered that there is great light among the injured living, and also great light when healing turns to death. The struggling animals at Sarvey taught me to love the here and now, to be mindful of each moment.

My first day at Sarvey was remarkable. I was given a small white bucket, disinfectant, and towels and told to clean the bird room. Suzy, my volunteer lead, then asked me to hold a bald eagle while she tube fed it. I nervously followed her into the med room where she taught me to hold the eagle's talons. It felt incredible. I learned to delicately cover its injured body and head with a towel – when eagles can't see, they can't harm themselves or anyone else.

Somehow I held the eagle's powerful body in my arms, shaking as we fed it fluids. I felt its beautiful, velvety wings and dinosaur-like talons between my fingers, together an exquisite work of art, and so perfectly made. As I helped Suzy put the eagle back into its cage, I thought about its life before injury and before Sarvey: flying through the skies, high above the trees with so much freedom. I had a strong sense that this eagle knew it was now time to trust us.

Suzy was a mother hen to the volunteers. She made sure that we were always learning something in exchange for our efforts. When the barred owl's heart stopped beating one Thursday afternoon on the med room table, Suzy looked at me and said, »At least he lived just one day in total freedom. That's more than most humans and many animals will ever know.«

In 2006 my father went blind. An amazing painter all his life, he lost his eyesight due to an undiagnosed disease. My sister and I began devoting our lives to his care. Although Sarvey remained a focus of my dedication and passions, my role of caregiver took on even deeper dimensions.

Soon after my father's diagnosis, there was Angel – a raven that arrived at the Center. From what we could deduce of her early life, she had likely fallen out of her nest as a baby when a man found her injured in the forest and brought her home. When Angel returned to health and her restive self, he chained both her legs inside a cage outdoors.

Angel had a nasty disposition from a life of mistreatment, but we quickly bonded. She had a giant personality and would hark her name, »Angel!« over and over, her voice sounding like the scratchy old man who took her from the forest. The staff at Sarvey knew that she would never fly again, so I was allowed to imprint – to become her friend. My bond with Angel reminded me of my mother. Angel and I would talk to each other while I held her and smoothed down her feathers. I felt that she came to Sarvey for me, and that I was there for her.

It was during my time with Angel in 2008 that I made my most memorable photographs. I would sit with her after I finished cleaning, and we would talk. She preened and posed for my photos, allowing me the time I needed to capture her complex personality. Angel taught me how to listen and speak to animals, to capture their spirits on film. Every wild thing has a soul full of strength, and my goal was to portray them like humans.

The lighting conditions at the Center were mostly fluorescent except for the skylight in the med room, so I started setting up my own lights. I taught myself a lot about cameras and lighting during that time, and this turned into a great period of artistic and professional development. More importantly, it was a time of personal growth and healing, working in harmony with the growth and healing of the animals I came to love.

In the winter of 2009, Sarvey had come to the difficult decision to put Angel to rest as she was no longer healing and had developed painful bumble foot in both feet. The outpouring of love from Angel's human friends was beautiful: My thoughtful neighbor Mike made her a cedar box while another volunteer, Robert, brought a red cloth to wrap her in as part of a Native American tradition. Robert also played his flute for her — something they had often shared together.

The morning of Angel's death was beautiful and sunny when we all gathered in the med room. Angel was on the floor with Robert and me when she suddenly jumped up onto the tall stool and then onto the med table. We couldn't believe it. With two bad legs and so much pain, she made it clear that she was ready to move on from this world. Just before her final moments, I looked into the forest through the skylight and saw a bald eagle in the tree above. As Angel's little body went limp, I looked up and saw that the eagle had flown away.

Eagles are known in Native American tradition to be the carriers of spirits back to the creator, and they are considered spiritual messengers between gods and humans by many cultures. It is said that if someone or something endures pain, the eagle signals a new beginning, providing the stamina and resilience to endure. That day, I believe the eagle came for both Angel and me.

Annie Marie Musselman

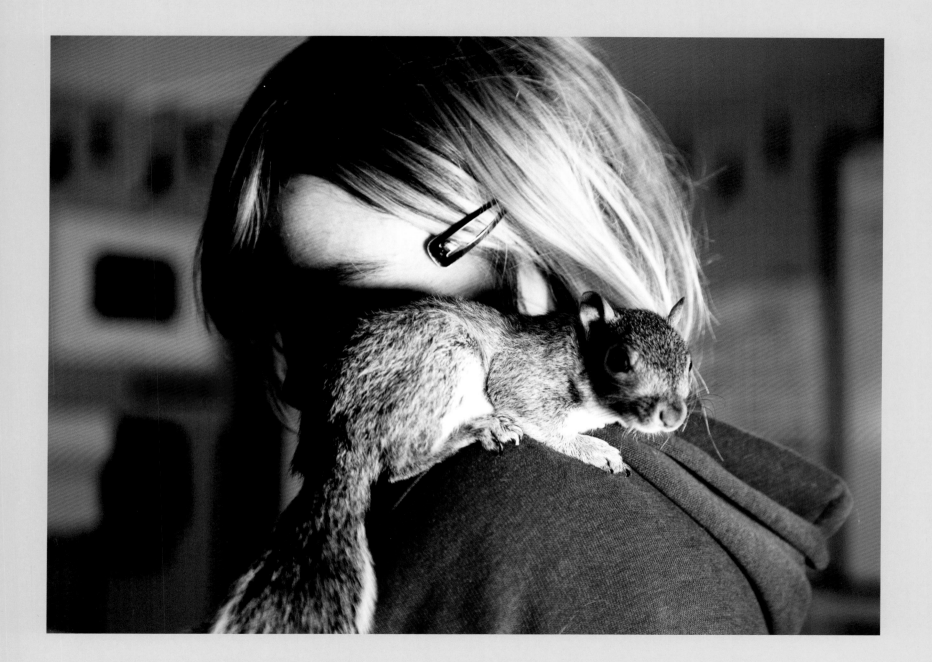

Annie with an Eastern Grey Squirrel